KT-453-098

IN LOVE
AND IN LAUGHTER

A PORTRAIT OF
ROBERT MACKIE

by Nansie Blackie

SAINT ANDREW PRESS

EDINBURGH

First published in 1995 by
SAINT ANDREW PRESS
121 George Street, Edinburgh EH2 4YN.

Copyright © Nansie Blackie 1995

ISBN 0 7152 0716 4

All rights reserved. No part of this publication may be reproduced or transmitted in any form or by any means, electronic or mechanical, including photocopy, recording, or information storage and retrieval system, without permission in writing from the publisher. This book is sold, subject to the condition that it shall not, by way of trade or otherwise, be lent, re-sold, hired out or otherwise circulated without the publisher's prior consent.

British Library Cataloguing in Publication Data
A catalogue record for this book
is available from the British Library.

ISBN 0 7152 0716 4

Cover design by Mark Blackadder.

Printed and **bound** in Great Britain by Bell & Bain Ltd, Glasgow.

Contents

Anthem

Let us praise our Maker, with true passion extol Him.
Let the whole creation give out another sweetness,
Nicer in our nostrils, a novel fragrance
From cleansed occasions in accord together
As one feeling fabric, all flushed and intact,
Phenomena and numbers announcing in one
Multitudinous oecumenical song
Their grand givenness of gratitude and joy,
Peaceable and plural, their positive truth
An authoritative This, an unthreatened Now
When, in love and in laughter, each lives itself,
For, united by His Word, cognition and power,
System and Order, are a single glory,
And the pattern is complex, their places safe.

~ W H AUDEN ~

*'He went through the world
expecting the son of God to pass.'*

~ KAY FENN ~

To JAMES CAMPBELL BLACKIE
~ sometime Chaplain to Edinburgh University
and Professor at New College ~
who shared Robert's
reconciling and humorous spirit.

Acknowledgements

IN response to pressure from many who worked in the ecumenical movement in this century, Jean Fraser embarked on a life of Robert Mackie some years ago, producing a summary account and collection of material. When her health did not allow her to continue, she passed this material on to William Perkins of the World Council of Churches. He undertook some interviewing, but preparations for the World Assembly of the WCC at Canberra gave him no time to continue. I am grateful to both for their generosity in allowing the fruit of their labours to become the starting point of my own.

I am also grateful to the staff of the WCC Archives, Geneva and the SCM Archives, Selly Oak, Birmingham for access and friendly assistance. A small fund for just such a purpose helped to make the Geneva visit possible. Most importantly, I am in debt to Steven and Annebeth Mackie for unrestricted access to the Mackie Papers.

Thanks are due to the SCM Press for permission to use brief extracts from the three titles enumerated in the text; to the late Mabel Small for references to her account *Growing Together*, and to Faber and Faber Ltd B.C. ex Canada, USA Random House for the use of W H Auden's poem 'Anthem' from the *Collected Poems* by W H Auden (E Mendelson, ed). I am particularly grateful to the editorial staff at Saint Andrew Press for their assistance.

So many of Robert's colleagues, friends and successors were willing to talk or write to me that it would be invidious to start to list their number and I apologise that I had not time to take advantage of all their offers.

Finally, I should acknowledge the patient and repeated corrections of my son Peter whose relationship with a word processor is so much more amicable than my own.

Foreword
by Lesslie Newbigin

THERE are at least two reasons for welcoming the publication of this book. In the first place, it makes an important contribution to the understanding of the history of Christianity in the latter part of this century. Those of us who have lived through this century have the remarkable privilege of living in the first century of Christian reunion. Most of the preceding centuries have been marked by quarrels among Christians which have resulted in schisms which seemed to be set in concrete. This century also has had its share of quarrels, but it has also seen an unprecedented movement of reunion. In spite of many disappointments, this remains a fact of immense significance. It has been in large part a product of the world-wide missionary movement which has also given this century the unique character of being the first in which it could truly be claimed that the Church is present in every nation. At the heart of both these developments was the rise a century ago of the Student Volunteer Missionary movement with its often criticised watchword: 'The Evangelization of the World in this Generation'. This phrase was not understood to refer to the conversion of the world in one generation; these early enthusiasts were not as stupid as that. They did believe, however, that it was possible for the whole world to be within reach of the Gospel in the space of one generation. And one can truly say that, if not in one generation, certainly in one century, their vision has come very near to realisation.

Robert Mackie's life and ministry were at the heart of this movement. As successively General Secretary of the British Student Christian Movement and the World's Student Christian

Federation, and then as a senior staff leader of the World Council of Churches during its formative years, he played a very important part in the formation and development of the ecumenical movement.

The second reason for commending this book is that it gives a faithful account of an exceptionally good and lovable Christian man. A close friend of Robert's – the late Eric Fenn – said to me that Nansie Blackie had taken on an impossible task, for Robert was just a very good man and how do you make someone who is 'just a very good man' sound interesting? I don't think I have met anyone who so completely removed himself from the centre of attention as Robert did. Not that you were conscious of anything like a deliberate action. It was just that he gave his whole attention to the people he was meeting and the subject in hand. I am finding it hard to express this. There was no trace of sentimentality in Robert. He cared deeply about people, and about the things which affect people's lives. He was – it seemed – wholly uninterested in himself. And, of course, he had a wonderfully infectious sense of humour – which I suppose is one of the real marks of a saint who knows that he is only a sinner saved by grace.

I think that Nansie Blackie has done this 'impossible' job splendidly and I hope that the book will be widely read – not only by Robert's friends who will need no urging, but by all who want to understand the story of Christianity in the present century.

Lesslie Newbigin
HERNE HILL
July 1995

Introduction

LISTENING recently to a youthful participant in the 1991 Canberra Assembly of the World Council of Churches (WCC) describing the problems and tensions within such a world church gathering, I was shaken to hear her suggest that it might be good if the World Council were closed down and the ecumenical movement started again from scratch. (Presumably the French Revolutionary leaders harboured similar fantasies when they introduced a completely new calendar starting with year 'One'.)

The suggestion was scarcely serious, but it revealed such a lack of historical perspective, so little appreciation of the efforts and sacrifices of the great twentieth century ecumenical pioneers – Athenagoras the First, George Bell, Eugene C Blake, Kathleen Bliss, Charles H Brent, Sarah Chakko, Paul Couturier, Suzanne de Dietrich, Germanos of Thyateira, Josef Hromadka, John XXIII, Toyohiko Kagawa, T Z Koo, Hendrik Kraemer, Hanns Lilje, John R Mott, Lesslie Newbigin, Martin Niemöller, D T Niles, Frederick Nolde, J H Oldham, William Paton, Nathan Soderblom, William Temple, Visser 't Hooft, Robert Mackie, Johannes Willebrands – sustained through and across two World Wars, the Cold War, imperialisms, nationalism, racism, ideologies and injustice, that my indignation rose on their behalf.

At which point I seemed to hear Robert laugh. He had a distinctive and infectious laugh, born of a secure faith and a sense of the ridiculousness of much human pretension – within the church and out of it. Lesslie Newbigin has written of 'that lilt in his voice which always suggested a bubble of laughter about to break the surface'. It is a laugh well remembered by an extraordinary number of people on every continent, many in positions of leadership in church, state, education and community – all of whom insist it was Robert Mackie who first saw their potential and gave them the opportunity to develop it. Robert himself wrote: 'Our natural escape from thought is indignation.'

The great enabler of others, modest to a fault, Robert Mackie would not have shared the perception of many of his friends and admirers that he was insufficiently appreciated when, 'perhaps the best known Scot outside Scotland' of his generation of churchmen, he concluded his work as Director of Inter-Church Aid and Associate General Secretary of the World Council of Churches and returned to Scotland from Geneva in 1955. The Reformed ecclesiastical tradition of which he was so comfortably a part has little place for honorary titles or positions, an attitude not always understood by those used to more hierarchical structures. An exception is the honorary Doctor of Divinity, and his old college, Trinity, made sure that Glasgow University gave him one of those.

Nothing could be less appropriate than to attempt to assess in any competitive way the significance of the fathers and mothers of ecumenism, but few would dispute the claim for Robert Mackie that none was better loved. That is itself a just reward, as love, unsentimental, costly, realistic, was at the heart of his theology and his life. It led him to accept tasks he did not like such as administration, and to live in places with no appeal for him such as London instead of Edinburgh, and Canada when Britain was at war, but always in a grace-full and humorous spirit.

The present stage of ecumenical commitment, as represented in Scotland by Action of Churches Together, has inevitably brought new difficulties along with new opportunities, as Gospel demands collide with ancient structures. We badly need in our leaders Robert's outstanding qualities of vision, patience and total conviction. He embodied the concept of 'enabling' leadership before the word had become fashionable, and indeed it could be argued that the concept has not in the intervening years moved much beyond the area of training theory. The principle of 'the priesthood of all believers' is today an integral part of the understanding of the nature of the church in all traditions, but its implications for practice under the weight of diverse historical institutions have hardly begun to be taken seriously. There is an uneasy fit between the seeming preference for the charismatic leader, in secular terms the appeal of a Napoleon or a Churchill, and the actions such as footwashing, or the teaching as in the Sermon on the Mount, of Jesus himself. It is all the more important that we honour and conserve the example of a man who worked at every level, Scottish, British and international, in a way which both got things done and empowered others in the process. Prisoners of our current preconceptions about church history, it seems all the more remarkable to us that he emerged from the background of an Edwardian Presbyterian manse in a small town in Scotland.

CHAPTER 1

Roots

THE beginning was in 1899, when a third child, a son, was born to the Reverend James Mackie, United Presbyterian minister in Bothwell, a small town about ten miles from the industrial city of Glasgow. Two daughters, Janette and Rhoda, were already seven and four years old, a sufficient difference to make them Robert's affectionate mentors rather than his childhood companions. A manse family in those days had strong and close bonds with the local community; it was a mutually accepted role of obligation and a certain measure of distance. Thus Robert was educated at home, mostly by his father, until he was nine years old: 'I learnt my numbers from the Church Hymnary.'[1]

From the start he grew up within the context of an explicit church tradition, learning to read under the gaze of a portrait of his father's honoured teacher, Dr John Cairns, who had been Principal of the United Presbyterian College in Edinburgh; he was a man who left behind no books but 'his zeal for the Gospel, his international Christian contacts, and his passion for unity'.[2]

After the age of nine Robert travelled every day into the city to Glasgow Academy, but a serious eye complaint three years later confined him to a darkened room for several months, cementing the bond with his father as teacher and friend: 'my early intimacy was never broken.'[3] The medical problem remained, however, involving the use of a glass eye from middle-age, an event so little remarked on by Robert himself that even the closest colleague could register shock at its casual removal during a theological discussion.

These circumstances allowed him to grow up without that degree of peer bonding which can have a negative effect on

1

relationships with age groups other than one's own; he was at ease with older people when he was young and with young people when he was old. It bred, moreover, a certain independence of mind and disregard of 'fashion' in ideas or attitudes. Looking back, Robert saw himself as having been in certain respects solitary as a young boy, although he said this without self-pity, an emotion with which he remained unfamiliar throughout his life.

The family background on both sides exhibits the classic Victorian and reputedly protestant characteristics of hard work, personal initiative, social mobility and eventual material reward. His maternal grandfather, James Cuthbert, son of a carrier from Ayr, started as a clerk in the Clyde Shipping Company and finished as a Director, to be succeeded in the firm by two of his sons. Robert had clear memories of visiting his widow in her rather splendid 'high Victorian villa ... with a turret and flagstaff' near Helensburgh on the banks of the firth of Clyde, and always 'retained the impression that no way of seeing the countryside could compare with sitting high up behind a pair of horses' [4] in company with the coachman.

As a day-boy at Glasgow Academy Robert frequented the West End home of a Cuthbert uncle who was a successful doctor, gaining a familiarity with an affluent Edwardian way of life in that mercantile city which survived the First World War only in a diminished form.

His paternal grandfather had also 'risen in the world', although not with such material benefits and in the context of a smaller community. Also called Robert Mackie, he was the son of a textile dyer who had come to Stewarton, another small town not far from Bothwell, from what was probably near subsistence farming in Galloway, that wild, beautiful and mountainous area of south-west Scotland, in the early years of the nineteenth century. With little schooling he took evening classes, and at the age of 22 set up his own bonnet-making business, building a small factory next to his father's workshop; two of his sons and a grandson followed him into the business. Taking a keen interest in local affairs, in time he became Provost of Stewarton, and the family tradition continued two generations later when his grand-daughter, Robert's sister Janette, became Provost of Lanark.

The choice of the ordained church ministry by Robert's father, James, would arise in part out of the strong sense of individual and social responsibility which characterised Scottish society at the time, but also out of a certain reaction to its competitive materialism and ambition. Not an overtly political person, it is revealing to see James writing to his son from his retirement during the Depression years of the 1930s: 'There must be some world co-operation of some kind, and perhaps a wise and broad socialism will have to be adopted.'[5]

At the same time, such a decision for the ministry was well respected and understood within the business community itself. It is significant that Robert's Uncle Cuthbert left him, his only clerical nephew, £250 instead of the £100 received by the others! Certainly, inequalities of wealth and privilege were always apparent and deplored by a boy nurtured in a home where Christian values were unashamedly practised as well as preached.

It was a natural response for Robert to be involved from his teens in the leadership of a boys' club and he retained an interest in the welfare of the individual boys long after he had left home. He was delighted to hear from his mother that the leader he had trained to follow him had soon demonstrated his independence: 'I was much afraid that I had created that great failure a one-man show.'[6]

Awareness of inequality, however, led him neither to complacency nor condescension, neither to envy nor judgement, but to sensitivity and responsibility. He seemed from his boyhood and throughout his life to have been able almost instinctively to develop from the particularities of circumstance the positive rather than the negative possibilities; the effect of his early solitariness provides only one example.

His father served the whole of his ministry in Bothwell – with faithfulness and fulfilment. Robert later wrote: 'He had no ambition to scholarship, nor indeed any ambition at all except to preach the Gospel and shepherd the lost. Most of his pastoral time was spent with people who never came to church.'[7] 'Home' for Robert, therefore, throughout his early life, included 'church' quite literally. Later he wrote:

Once I heard a school friend say to another, 'You should come out with us to Mackie's. There's a church in his garden'. And that was quite a good description of the big stone manse, and the little church on the slope beyond the willow-tree and the washing-green .... The little church was domesticated .... Yet it kept its dignity for me; I had been baptised in it, I entered full communion in it, I was ordained in it.[8]

He was sad to find it virtually derelict when he visited it in his eighties; he rescued a piece of broken stained glass and a fallen stone to preserve in Croftlands, the retirement house he had inherited from his father.

'Church' was to remain 'home' for him, but a larger, wider 'church'. Intimations were there from the beginning: 'Looking out from my window I could see through the trees the gaunt half-deserted tenement in which David Livingstone had been born.'[9] Coincidentally, his sister, Rhoda, was to marry Livingstone's grandson, Hubert Wilson.

One of the genuine advantages of Reformed church polity, with its parity of ministry, is the priority it gives to the parish ministry on a life-time basis without the distraction of hierarchical possibilities or any kind of ecclesiastical careerism. The example of his father, and later his father-in-law, George Steven, gave Robert a lasting model of Christian vocation which freed him from any kind of clerical ambition; it was an irony of circumstance that took him to so many posts and places.

Although Bothwell was at that time a mining town, James Mackie's parishioners ranged from 'well-to-do business people to miners with a precarious existence and income'[10]; it lay in a rural setting, preserving a strong sense of its own identity in spite of the economic dominance of its encroaching neighbour, Glasgow. Robert retained a life-long loyalty to both. Now as then, geo-graphical and historical factors have enabled most Scottish small towns to escape the insidious process of suburbanisation which has undermined community life in many parts of the developed world. The sense of local community remained strong in Robert, and its absence in a life of travel based on London, Toronto and Geneva was one of the genuine deprivations he bore with patience and cheerfulness. It was to assuage this frustration that he chose Biggar, another small Lanarkshire town roughly equidistant from Edinburgh and Glasgow, as his home for the last years of his life, when the condition of his wife's health might have suggested Edinburgh as a more suitable location. The distinctive hill, Tinto, which neighbours Biggar, can actually be seen from Bothwell.

The countryside itself became and remained an essential part of Robert's life and his appreciation of the world around him. It was a walked, climbed, known countryside, not merely a landscape admired from a distance or from a car. Indeed, his father did not drive, and in the early days access to a car for parochial purposes was available only as a gift from his father-in-law. This was used to hire regular drivers who, typically, became family friends. Hill-walking was not only his father's chief leisure pursuit, but also a pleasure widely shared in the Scotland of the 1920s and 30s. All through his life, in his often abbreviated leisure time, Robert would take to hill-walking in Switzerland, in Scotland, or wherever he found himself; this was for him the essence of a holiday. The strength of his affection for such a context and for outdoor activity shows the discipline he required of himself to accept a regimen of long office hours, chair-bound travel, committee meetings and administration. When we include an understanding of his eye trouble, we become aware of natural predeliction and physical disability ignored.

The appreciation of natural beauty ...

> ... *a sense sublime*
> *Of something far more deeply interfused,*
> *Whose dwelling is the light of setting suns,*
> *And the round ocean and the living air,*
> *And the blue sky, and in the mind of man ....* [11]

permeated his attitude to the world and his understanding of creation. From his 1928 diary comes: 'Can anyone understand the Bible who has not a deep true appreciation of nature and the countryside?' It was romanticism, but a romanticism of depth, genuinely poetic – the romanticism of sentiment not of sentimentality.

Robert shared his enthusiasm for hill-walking and, in some cases, a similar attitude to nature with several of his elders and contemporaries such as Barth, Bonhoeffer, Paton and Newbigin. At the Vancouver 1933 World Council of Churches (WCC) General Assembly a later generation articulated this more clearly when they brought environmental concern, 'the integrity of creation', to the centre of ecumenical thinking.

'Received wisdom' about Scottish Presbyterianism at the beginning of the twentieth century, or perhaps merely popular secular prejudice, would raise expectations of authoritarianism and restrictiveness in regard to the family life of the clergy, but none of this was true of the Mackie manse. It was here that Robert developed his attitude to the Bible which was to inform his life and, through him, the lives of thousands of others. He wrote:

> *For my father's generation, it was a new, exciting and expanding Bible. Modern biblical criticism had won its victory and has opened up the Scriptures. It had not undermined faith, it had given faith a fresh and convincing basis.*[12]

A colleague from his time as General Secretary to the British Student Christian Movement (SCM) wrote decades later: 'Chiefly I remember those many occasions at the end of a conference or gathering when you took up our concerns and put them into the context of a passage from the Bible and in doing so laid our lives open in the presence of God'.[13]

Robert recorded that his father never discussed 'church unity' as a topic, but exhibited it always in his life. He was a friend both of the local Free Church minister and of the Roman Catholic priest, a position much less common in times when the 'Orange Movement', supporting Northern Irish presbyterianism, was very strong in the west of Scotland. On one occasion he publicly opposed the introduction of opening prayers at the meeting of the local School Board on discovering that the proposer's main motive was to keep the Roman Catholic priest waiting in the corridor.

There was nothing of a need to rebel in Robert's make-up. He never seems to have felt the necessity to react against family,

society, country or convention; at the same time he was mani-
festly not a prisoner to any of these. Somehow his security, his
identity, his faith, were so fundamentally rooted that he was able to
develop an extraordinary capacity to be open to those of other
temperaments, to rebels and to radicals, to those from other
cultures and church traditions, without feeling any compulsion to
identify with or dismiss their opinions. His close colleague and
friend, Eric Fenn, described it as a quite particular quality of
'detachment'.

In his nineties, Eric recalled sitting in a garden at a World's
Christian Student Federation (WSCF) meeting in Bad Boll,
Germany in 1932, watching Nazi recruits in the street beyond.
The rest of the group erupted in alarmed political debate; Robert
watched in silence.[14] The watching silence is partly filled by his
own separate account of the same incident:

> It was glorious spring weather, and we often sat in a wide circle in the
> garden ... [by] a highway along which groups of singing young
> people passed incessantly. Many carried banners – some with Christian
> symbols, some with Communist, some with national socialist symbols.
> As we read our Bibles and discussed the Gospel we were pledged to
> proclaim, we could not keep our eyes off this stream of young people.
> Where were they going? Where was Europe going? Where were we
> going? I have a vivid memory of our closing worship. It was led by
> Reinhold von Thadden[15] and by Pierre Maury.[16] The theme was: 'We
> are more than conquerors through him that loved us.'

There was, indeed, no lack of concern on the part of Robert,
for by his own choice he was to spend his life working in the eye
of the storm – the international arena. Davis McCaughey[17] writes,
'we knew that your relative detachment from passing fashions was
due not to indifference but to the strong attachment you had to
God and his purposes'.[18]

Numerous letters from many countries and from several generations, written on his retirement from the World Council of
Churches or for his eightieth birthday celebration, pay tribute to
his talent for listening, not judging, enabling others to develop and
to learn a new style of leadership themselves. This capacity went

beyond the ability to see many sides to a question intellectually, although he could do that.

Hans-Ruedi Weber[19] writes: 'This precious gift of yours, this "charisma" of giving confidence, we shall miss most ....' It included a remarkable empathy with alien feelings and perspectives and a concentration of concern that led very different types of characters to know themselves accepted, understood and encouraged. The required combination of imagination and understanding seems to bear some resemblance to that necessary characteristic of the poet, defined by Keats as 'negative capability'. In both cases the essential receptivity implies a source from without.

To put it in explicitly theological terms: Robert was a creature of 'Grace'.

Notes to Chapter 1

1   Manuscript notes, undated: Mackie Papers, Edinburgh.
2   Ibid.
3   Ibid.
4   Manuscript reminiscences, February 1978: ibid.
5   Letter from James to Robert Mackie, 27.9.1931: ibid.
6   Letter from Robert to his mother, 27.7.1924: ibid.
7   Manuscript notes, undated: ibid.
8   'Growing up in the Church': ibid.
9   Ibid.
10   Manuscript notes, undated: ibid.
11   'Lines composed a few miles above Tintern Abbey': William Wordsworth. His attitude closely reflects that of his wife, Dorothy, when she wrote of Wordsworth to her father from Cambridge, 29.1.1921: 'I feel somehow that I have more in common with him than with about any other man of genius.'
12   Manuscript notes, undated: Mackie Papers.
13   Letter from Davis McCaughey to Robert, 20.4.1979 – eightieth birthday tributes: ibid.
14   Interview with Eric and Kay Fenn, July 1991.
15   Reinhold von Thadden-Trieglaff, German SCM leader and initiator of the post-war Kirchentag movement.

16 Pierre Maury, French SCM leader.

17 J Davis McCaughey, post-war Study Secretary to the British SCM, later Professor and Principal of Ormond College, Melbourne and Governor of the state of Victoria.

18 Letter to Robert, 20.4.1979, from Davis McCaughey – eightieth birthday tributes: Mackie Papers.

19 Hans-Ruedi Weber, Director of the WCC Department of the Laity and later of Biblical Studies: Mackie Papers.

CHAPTER 2

Leaving Home

THE first experience of leaving home, both the manse and Scotland, came when Robert was 17; after one and a half years of a Glasgow University Arts course he was sent as an officer cadet to Cambridge for six months at the end of 1917. It was a cultural shift of some magnitude and his letters give us ready access to his feelings and reactions. Indeed, the frequency with which Robert wrote to his mother, letters shared with his father, and her preservation of them, is not only evidence of the closeness and openness of his family relationships, but brings also an invaluable intimacy to the record.

He begins with many normal boyish prejudices: 'The language is indeed strange here to our ears .... The flat country get on one's nerves ....' At the same time he responds unaffectedly to beauty ... the crocuses in early spring ... King's College Chapel is 'easily the most wonderful' he has seen. Alien Anglican forms of worship provoke adolescent unease at first: 'we chanted all manner of evil things of colossal length.' From some unexpressed inner compulsion, however, he perseveres in regular attendance at the worship of other traditions, in tandem with his faithful adherence to the presbyterian St Columba's congregation. Soon he writes of the King's College liturgy: 'I shall never see a more beautiful service'; and again, of Ely Cathedral Evensong, 'Never have I been at a service which filled me more with reverence and appreciation'.[1]

Perhaps the historical persistence of the principle '*ecclesia semper reformanda*' has granted a particular freedom of self-criticism without disloyalty to those who stand within what is called the 'Reformed' tradition. This inherited cast of mind may in part explain the leading role which that tradition has played in the early development of ecumenical organisations. If this is so, it is all the less easy to understand the inflexibility of some of the branches of the same tradition for whom the adjective 'reformed' would seem to be irretrievably locked into the past tense. At the same time, it has possibly made it the more difficult for 'the reformed' to understand, in the last resort, those for whom criticism of the church as institution is shadowed by ancient taboo. There is no evidence, however, that Robert himself experienced this difficulty in, for example, his pioneering work amongst Orthodox students in the World Student Christian Federation (WSCF). From the beginning he had a huge capacity for acceptance.

In spite of the demands of his own course, he took every oppor-tunity at Cambridge to hear scholars in different disciplines. He tells his father that a lecture on animism is 'the very best lecture I have ever heard .... He brought out the point that Christ's coming did not break the sequence of religion'.[2] The tone suggests a shared positive approach to pre-Christian religion, not a commonplace attitude within evangelical protestantism of the day, but already emerging within British missionary writing.[3]

In view of a more famous occasion a generation later, when a fellow Scot, Eric Liddell, refused to run on a Sunday during the Olympic Games, Robert's thinking over a similar problem reveals a less individualistic approach to Christian ethics. He too had been brought up in a sabbatarian tradition which he had seen no reason to reject. He had taken up rowing, but not on a Sunday. Offered a team place which would involve occasional Sunday practice, he at first refused. With genuine courtesy the captain offered to make an exception and give him a team place without the Sunday practices. After considerable thought Robert decided that this would be to make the other members pay for his scruples and he accepted the place without the concession – an early instance of 'situation ethics'. It is an odd but persistent characteristic of many twentieth century secularists that they admire most, from a safe distance, consistency and even rigidity in what they see as religious principles; Liddell is known and admired far more for this sabbatarian stand than for his later self-sacrifice in China. It would seem that both Christians and non-Christians continue to have great difficulty in coming to terms with the radical non-legalism of Jesus' ethical teaching.

After six months at Cambridge, Robert was posted to France in the summer of 1918 as a Second Lieutenant in the Highland Light Infantry (HLI), attached to the third Labour Company. He was in charge of men regarded in the army hierarchy as 'bottom of the heap' in class and function. His reaction appears in his letters: 'The Major thinks we can make nothing of the men we have .... I disagree.'[4] He was both angry on their behalf and sympathetic to their attitudes. In his supervision of making roads and digging ditches in all weathers, his scout leader's experience with the Bothwell boys must have proved more useful than the Cambridge musketry lectures. He was appalled to discover that, in such conditions, many men had only one shirt. 'Some of them have even got the boots off the dead.'[5] His mother responded swiftly by organising parcels from the Bothwell community.

Robert made determined efforts to get on well with his fellow officers, but the nature of his concern for his men caused him to have different priorities: 'I have my own idea of my duties.'[6] Early on he disobeys orders so that he may get to know them individually.

Uncomfortable with officer privilege, he destroys one of his own letters home expressing some grievance because he knows that such complaints are censored out of the men's letters. Still only 18, he undertook such censorship duties in a wholly pastoral spirit, much moved by the religious tone of many. The armistice declared, he appreciates the decline in the men's motivation and scrounges a football, setting up Sports and Amusement Committees and, made Education Officer, introduces classes in English, French, maths and history. Lacking co-operation from other officers and at his wits' end for materials, he sends home for his old text-books and does most of the teaching himself, whilst at the same time encouraging hidden talent in, for example, a sergeant with shorthand.

In microcosm, then, we see the future man: the realistic assessment of the situation, the desire to humanise it, the enabling of others and the willingness to accept the drudgery most avoided, all with enthusiasm and amused self-deprecation.

He had a habit of approaching working parties on foot instead of on the usual horseback, to give the men time to get back to work if they had been taking a break. He wrote of poor attendance at classes during the weary wait for demobilisation: 'As the men have no work to do, they do not attend well. They only come when it means getting out of something.'[7] In the officers' mess he had the moral courage to toast the King's health in water, but was not moralistic about different attitudes to alcohol: 'some people seem to get the fullest enjoyment that way.'[8]

This lack of moralism foreshadows a frequently reported incident from his later travels for Inter-Church Aid; in the early 1950s he went with a group of Protestant church leaders (all 'non-drinkers') to an impoverished Mediterranean village where their gratitude could only be expressed through an offer of the local wine. Robert having been the one member of the party to accept the drink, he was reproached afterwards by the rest for lack of principle: 'someone had to be Christian,' he said. As in so many areas, Robert Mackie seems intuitively to have adopted without fuss or fervour a prioritising of values within Christian behaviour which downgraded the particularities of ecclesiastical and national conditioning, without ever abandoning the structures of a necessary self-discipline which these provide.

During these few months in France, Robert took the opportunity to befriend local people who were returning refugees, a situation to be strangely reversed in 1941 when he and his family were briefly 'lost' during the German occupation. In 1918 he writes:

> *As well as being a sort of labour boss I am, curiously enough, an interpreter and general agent for refugees. I do all the liaison work between the billeters and the billetees ...*[9]

– oddly prophetic of the remit of the future Director of Inter-Church Aid and Refugee Service.

In a typical blend of realism and modesty, he concludes in one of his last letters in 1919: 'I have not been a great success as an officer but I think I have not been a failure ....'[10] At the same time, however, his batman writes to Mrs Mackie, 'I could not wish to serve under a better officer'.[11]

Although he longed to get back to his University course,

Robert had refused to pursue his own demobilisation with any vigour, feeling that it was only fair that 'last in' should be 'last out'. For the rest of his life he owned to a feeling of guilt that the chance factor of a year or so of age had spared him the suffering and death which had faced his immediate seniors, 'burdened with a sense of shame because I had come so late and done so little.' [12] This served later to reinforce his discomfort that the work of General Secretary of the WSCF demanded his absence from Britain during the Second World War.

Notes to Chapter 2

1   Letters to mother from Cambridge, January–June 1918: Mackie Papers, Edinburgh.
2   Ibid.
3   For example, William Paton's *Jesus Christ and the World's Religions* appeared in 1916 as an SCM study book, became a bestseller and only went out of print in 1956.
4   Letters to mother from France, October 1918/January 1919: Mackie Papers.
5   Ibid.
6   Ibid.
7   Ibid.
8   Ibid.
9   Ibid.
10   Ibid.
11   Letter to Mrs Mackie from Sergeant, 14.2.1919: ibid.
12   Letter to mother from France, 1918: ibid.

CHAPTER 3

New Horizons

IN 1982 Robert wrote of his return from the war:

> *In October 1919 I stood on the staircase leading up to matriculation office in Glasgow University. I had been asked to act that morning as agent for the SCM or the Christian Union as we called our branch. I had been a member for three years, but the war had taken me away for a year and a half. All I had to do was to give out a leaflet and an invitation to 'social'. But one man ... began to ask me questions .... Indifference I had expected but for questioning I was not prepared .... It was then that I realised that the SCM was not a normal function for students, but a step out of line. In the ordinary world the Church – in some form or other – did religion ... but here in the student world some of us found that we had to do religion for ourselves and find our way into a developing faith with the help of our friends ... we knew that nothing human was foreign to the Gospel.*[1]

Here was an atmosphere in which the concerns and perspectives already evident in the youthful Highland Light Infantry officer found ready acceptance and opportunity for challenge and growth.

It is not, however, possible to appreciate what Robert received from and gave to the Student Christian Movement without understanding something about its history and character. Its origins lie most obviously in the evangelical movements of the nineteenth century, more specifically in their effect on the missionary outlook of individual students, notably on groups from Oxford, Cambridge, Edinburgh, Glasgow, St Andrews, Dublin and Aberystwyth. The impact in the 1890s of the slogan 'the evangelisation of the world in this generation', brought to British universities by the Americans

John R Mott[2] and Robert Wilder[3], was of an order difficult to imagine now after a further hundred years of secularisation. With hindsight, there is considerable significance in the phrase 'evangelisation of the world', where a concern for society might be seen to temper the strong individualistic bias of much nineteenth century evangelicalism. John R Mott explains the thinking behind his emphasis on the importance of students in his foreword to Ruth Rouse's history of the World Student Christian Federation (WSCF):

> *The universities and colleges of the world teach the teachers, preach to the preachers, and govern the governors. Therefore, well may we go with Elisha, 'to the spring of the waters and cast the salt in there'.*[4]

The British Council of Christian Unions had been one of the five founders of the Federation in 1895. Something of the geographical range of the latter is suggested by the locations of its major meetings, such as Tokyo in 1907, Constantinople in 1911, Lake Mohonk, USA in 1913, Peking in 1922. It survived the traumatic divisions of war; in some ways it was even strengthened by an appreciation of failure: R O Hall, later to be the first Anglican bishop to ordain women priests in Hong Kong in 1942, reported back to the British SCM as its representative in Peking:

> *The Mohonk Conference had broken up in a spirit of great optimism and international goodwill, and its members set out as they thought to build a new world at once. Actually they set out to kill each other singing the same hymns, and praying for victory to the same God.*[5]

By 1924 the only European countries without Federation members were Iceland, Lithuania, Albania and Spain.

Robert then, handing out his invitations on the Glasgow stair, was opening the door not merely to a local fellowship, but also to what was already a world family, characterised by a mutual concern for shared problems and for the care of overseas students in the home context. An example of this had been the creation by the Glasgow SCM of the International Club in 1916. Tissington Tatlow, the formidable and far-sighted Anglican cleric who was

General Secretary of the British SCM from 1898 to 1900 and 1903 to 1929, was concerned that the SCM, which was not itself a church, should nevertheless be seen and supported as an instrument for the inspiration and education of those who would become faithful, but not uncritical, members of the churches of the future. The adoption in 1898 of the term 'inter-denominational' rather than 'undenominational' to describe the SCM, signalled this acceptance of the centrality of 'church' both theologically and practically. He was anxious, therefore, to draw speakers and advisors (Senior Friends), locally and nationally, from the whole spectrum of theological and ecclesiastical tradition.

Several factors combined to give much greater importance to a strong student-led Christian organisation within the field of higher education than can easily be appreciated in the 1990s. These include the significant place of both church and university in British society and the largely accepted concept of an elite student class, although there were significant differences here between the Oxbridge and the Scottish and English 'redbrick' academic traditions. In the 1920s and 1930s the SCM often provided leadership in general student affairs, in unions and Student Representative Councils, and the emergence of both the National Union of Students and the International Students' Service owes much to its initiative. There grew up several generations of academic staff who had known and trusted each other in this context, however much their later perspectives may have diverged. Still more evidently, within the leadership of denominations, there emerged those who had shared so much during university and theological training that church divisions in later life became an affront to personal fellowship and not merely a matter of individual theological conviction. Thus, for the inter-war period in Britain, what the SCM thought today the churches often thought tomorrow, as, in the natural progression of things, SCM staff (rather misleadingly called 'Secretaries') moved on to become Bishops, Board Conveners and executives of missionary societies.

By 1919, when Robert's real involvement began, the original evangelical and missionary character of the SCM had not diminished, but widened and deepened. The markedly religious dimension to British nineteenth century society, observed as singular by the French historian Halévy, had given birth to a great range of movements and endeavours: Anglo-Catholicism, Christian Socialism, the Scottish Disruption, militant non-conformity, the Salvation Army, amongst others. The driving force behind the emancipation of slaves, prison reform, child protection, Gladstonian Liberalism, trade unionism, the Labour Party, even public health, was more often than not explicitly Christian. At the same time the nature and growing authority of scientific attitudes brought about profound changes in the intellectual climate and demanded new responses from both individuals and established institutions. The development of historical scholarship in its modern form had far-reaching implications both for Biblical criticism and for churches in their diverse historical particularity.

National and local SCM archives yield abundant evidence that the SCM's response to these multiple considerations, compounded by the trauma of the 1914–1918 war, was for it to become increasingly inclusive and open in approach to this and subsequent generations of students. 'Seeking the truth' appears frequently in the records as the specific vocation of the student, at whatever academic level senior or junior, and criticism was seen as a necessary method for the search. The place of Christian conviction was never minimised as foundation or goal, but honesty was always envisaged as a necessary virtue. If all truth came from God, it was an integral part of such a conviction that no truth could lead away from him. It is clear that it was frequently the women students who took the lead in the establishment of this attitude: Edinburgh women, in particular, resisted the imposition of a doctrinal test for membership at a time when increasingly students lacked a church family background. It would, however, also be true to say that women in higher education in the 1920s still constituted something of a pioneering group in every respect.

During this post-war period the continuing 'social concern' with poverty and privilege, not least in Glasgow, developed from a somewhat individualistic and moralistic approach to a more thorough analysis of the structure of society and an appreciation of the need for radical change. Where once overseas and domestic issues, the missionary and the 'social', had sometimes been seen as in competition in terms of vocation, now problems at home and abroad, peace, poverty, racism and injustice were seen to belong together. Looking back in 1982 Robert wrote:

> ... *the immediate world concern that really affected my generation was the discovery that our European fellow students – in Russia, in Eastern Europe and in Germany – were in deep poverty and distress. There was a crowded meeting in the Union to decide whether we would take part in European Student Relief. There was opposition, but a majority decision to do so. This was a challenge which it was not easy to meet after the bitterness of war. Gradually there arose a new sense of solidarity with our fellow students. We went round business premises asking for ... surplus clothing. To the Glasgow 1921 Conference we each brought an extra pair of shoes to send to ... European Student Relief .... In our own University we found overseas students who widened our horizons. I well remember a Chinese medical student startling a small group in active discussion by saying: 'The trouble about you people is that you cannot escape from your Christian background!' We realised suddenly the limits of our experience and the weakness of our judgements. We had so much to learn.*[6]

That realisation was to stay with Robert, and the capacity to learn was his to the end of his days.

It was, therefore, into a ferment of ideas in church and society, and into that microcosm of both which was the SCM, that Robert moved during his university years in Glasgow. By the end of them, in 1922, he emerged as student Chairman of the General Committee, the central legislative body of the whole British movement. Typically, the evidence reveals, he emerged gradually, through listening, learning and being receptive to others and to new ideas. He won respect and trust from churchmen of very different traditions – not by any means an easy achievement in those less ecumenical days.

'The Student Volunteer Movement' had been at the heart of the SCM since its origin; 'Student Volunteers' subscribed to a specific promise: 'It is my purpose, if God permit, to devote my life to missionary service abroad.'

Reared in a church tradition which laid considerable emphasis on such service, and on the theological concept of 'a call', it is not therefore surprising to discover Robert subscribing to the promise soon after returning to his studies. Whilst in France he had written that he did not know what he would do after University, but, given the depth of his Christian conviction and the example of his father, the future was always seen in terms of Christian vocation of some kind. This, for him, was satisfyingly 'normal' in its most profound sense and involved no 'Damascus road' type of experience. Indeed, Robert claimed that he only once made a major decision between two courses of action – in 1925, between work in India or for the SCM; on all other occasions he thought, listened to advice, waited on events, and prayed, until one course seemed inevitable. On occasion in the future he was to voice concern as to his fidelity to the Student Volunteer promise; a multitude of others, however, from every continent, give testimony to his good faith and to the peculiar appropriateness that the spirit of the age lent to the precise form of his 'missionary service abroad'.

At that stage in the development of missionary partnership, such a commitment by a man involved training either for ordination or for medicine; for Robert, with his abilities and temperament, it led to the three year Divinity course at Trinity College, Glasgow in preparation for ordination. It also made him respond to a letter in the church magazine from Dr J M Macphail asking for some-one to go out to the Jharia Coalfield in India for four months to experiment with the idea of a Coalfield Chaplaincy. This would involve an interruption, although an enrichment, to his academic studies. 'I was the only applicant, and I got the job ... the Indian visit did much more to prepare me for my life-work than my three years at a Theological College.'[7]

It is characteristic that he saw his acceptance in terms of a lack of competition rather than as an indication of his own peculiar capacity to respond to the new – for this was long before industrial chaplaincy became an accepted form of ministry in the 1950s.

His letters to his family on the sea voyage through the Suez Canal to India, the first of so many long journeys which were to be demanded of him, are now supplemented by others to Dorothy Steven, a Scottish SCM colleague, later to become his wife. This lends a more contemporary and SCM context to his comments. They illustrate with considerable clarity how he used such occasions: the appreciation of nature, of new countries, the opportunities made to talk and share with people from quite different backgrounds and experience, the seeking out of common points of contact, the disciplined reading, the practice of the presence of God.

He quotes Rupert Brooke:

> 'There are waters blown by changing winds to laughter ... and lit by the rich skies all day ....' The majesty of the sea, and the fact that I have no practical duties, force me to find God near at hand with a power that is for living more than for doing .... We are passing some islands ... known as the Twelve Apostles. There seems to be a poor lost Judas far out from all the rest.[8]

He befriends a Swiss lady's maid who comes from Herisau, which he had visited for a WSCF conference the previous year; also the Berwickshire valet to Lord Farringdon. He lends G K Chesterton's *St Francis* to a Roman Catholic nurse and reads her copy of Abbé Fouard's *Life of Christ* in return; he discovers an Indian student who is familiar with Student Movement House in London, the SCM centre for overseas students built in memory of those who had died in the war, and, by the end of the voyage, Robert is invited to visit him in Delhi. His reactions to his surroundings were not, however, invariably romantic – 'Gibraltar was for all the world the image of Dumbarton on a thoroughly bad day.'[9] There is an unselfconscious but determined effort to make use of the time, and to exercise his undoubted talent for friendship, which was to bear fruit in his unique contribution to the ecumenical movement in later years.

In more than one respect Indian independence, and the issues associated with it, seem to have occupied the place in British student attitudes in the 1920s that South Africa and apartheid were to have fifty years later – with Gandhi the Nelson Mandela of his day. The SCM, not least in Glasgow, had pioneered work amongst overseas students of any or no faith, and unease about the ambiguous relationship between colonialism and past missionary endeavour had helped to radicalise opinion. It is all the more marked, therefore, how Robert's approach to the situation and the people in

Jharia was both non-ideological and non-judgemental: 'I shall know more about India when I return, but I shall be less willing to give an opinion.'

On arrival at Pokhuria, and travelling round remote villages, he was immediately drawn to the Santals:

Life is gentle and sweet to the Santals, and it seems an intolerable shame that the coal mines should bribe them away from the jungle to drab townships.

The disturbance of their community traditions undermined 'the sacredness of ... [their] whole scheme of life'. He did not, however, dismiss the efforts of many of the mine managers to behave with fairness and concern: 'SCM folk don't do our simple, self-educated, hard-headed ... countrymen justice.'

An example of the complexity of the clash of cultures occurred whilst he was there, when the response of the Indian miners to the introduction of a ban on children working underground was to strike:

There has been much for me to learn about the different sets and opinions of the 200-300 Europeans in the coalfield .... Part of my difficulty is in being regarded as a padre. I have found one man – Mason, from near home – a Socialist, who treats me like a decent but foolish young man. He will be a great comfort.

He was particularly aware of the needs of those Scots who had married Indians and who were caught between two cultures. ·

Listening to a debate on the future of Europeans in India, he was impressed by the local Indian Civil Service official 'quoting the words of Jesus as the rule for India: "He that is greatest among you shall be the servant of all" .... He was cheered ... but I am afraid only a small percentage agreed'. Included in that percentage was the agent in charge of several collieries, Heron, who believed in that view 'to the hilt and is not afraid to say so. I never saw a man so fierce for justice and truth'.[10]

For Robert Mackie, the Gospel had unarguably what has come to be called 'a bias to the poor', but he never underestimated what numerous individuals at any one time and place did, patiently and variously, to practise Gospel values as they saw them. His capacity to understand how others could, from their different experience and contexts, hold different views, often kept him silent: 'I wonder how much aggressiveness is necessary for a Christian.'[11]

It was to be his lot, not always a happy one, to affirm pastoral values within a context – the ecumenical and the student arena where the prophetic is often more highly regarded. Should the Church 'curse the world or comfort it?', he wrote from India in 1925. Self-doubt, the feeling that he ought to be as convinced as his colleagues that he was right in political, social and theological matters, accompanied him throughout his life. His admirers, from Toronto to Nanjing, came to see that his particular qualities of imagination, understanding and pastoral concern were often in shorter supply amongst church leaders than self-confident certainty.

Of one conclusion Robert was in no doubt by the end of his summer in India: 'it is the love in a man's heart that counts.' He was full of admiration for 'the hard and very often dull work of a missionary's life ... [done] ... well and gladly'[12] by his host and guide, Hamilton, whose idea the coalfield chaplaincy had been. He was asked to return to take up the job on a more permanent basis, but resources for it still had to be found. He determined not to make any decision until he had arrived home, but felt that, if the work needed doing and he was wanted, his doubts about its frustrations and limitations were irrelevant. These humble but somewhat unusual criteria remained determinative of Robert's attitude to vocational choice for the rest of his life. In the meantime, however, others had different demands to make.

Notes to Chapter 3

1   'One man's experience of the SCM', 1982: Mackie Papers, Edinburgh.

2   American Methodist layman, indefatigable ecumenical pioneer for the WSCF and the YMCA, unique Honorary President of the new WCC in 1948.

3   One of the Princeton founders of the Student Volunteer Movement.

4   *The World's Student Christian Federation*, Ruth Rouse: SCM Press. In later years the name 'World Student Christian Federation' was adopted.
5   SCM Archives: Selly Oak Colleges' Library, Birmingham.
6   'One man's experience of the SCM', 1982: Mackie Papers.
7   Ibid.
8   Letters from India, 1924 and 1925: Mackie Papers.
9   Ibid.
10 Ibid.
11 Ibid.
12 Ibid.

CHAPTER 4

The SCM Commitment

ON his return home, the leadership of the SCM, both in Scotland and in the United Kingdom, combined to advocate the claims of full-time work with the Movement as Scottish Secretary. The General Secretary, Tissington Tatlow, wrote of Robert to the senior Scottish churchman with oversight of the Indian project: 'He is the outstanding figure for British students of his generation' [1]; and to Robert himself: 'It is absolutely vital to the continued existence of the Student Movement ... in Scotland in any form worth having, that you should accept.' [2]

In this instance Robert had no doubts at all about the value of the work to be done, only, as usual, some hesitation about his own abilities: 'I am rather a "goat" on accounts and the less I have to record the better ... I don't know how to make speeches ... much worse than sermons!' [3] This, from the man who became the outstanding first post-war Director of Inter-Church Aid, pre-eminent Editor of the WSCF's *The Student World* and expert communicator on a global scale! In retrospect he remarks, 'I had no creative ideas of my own. I was simply taken up in a movement far bigger in every way than I was, and used by it'. He saw himself as having been naively idealistic and propelled into maturity by colleagues and the passage of events. [4] He never seems to have appreciated how his extraordinary receptivity – his Keatsian 'negative capability' – was itself a particular talent, a talent which was the source of his style of leadership, attracting others and releasing their potential.

It is clear from his comments at the time and later, that he had come increasingly to find in the SCM that place where church and world met; where, in the aftermath of world war, the demands of peace, poverty and inequality were felt on the pulses; where the challenges of scientific thinking and Biblical criticism were taken seriously – all this within a rich diversity of historical church tradition and personal Christian commitment. A typical example of perspicacity in the contemporary political arena emerges from an editorial in *The Student Movement* (the British SCM periodical) in response to the terms of the Peace Treaty in May 1919: 'taken as a whole, the document lacks idealism or any traces of the spirit of reconciliation or magnanimity.'

First, however, he had to return to Glasgow and finish his theological training. Throughout his university career – interrupted as it was by the war and the Indian venture – Robert participated fully in all aspects of student life. He was prominent in student government, traditionally a particular feature in the Scottish academic scene, becoming President of the Students' Representative Council. He took a leading part in such diverse activities as drama and rowing. Nor did he turn his back on his local community, Bothwell, where he still lived: in March 1922 he found time to play Theseus in the Bothwell Literary Association's production of 'A Midsummer Night's Dream'. All these activities made him well-known and liked far beyond the bounds of the SCM, and gathered around him a group of friends who kept in contact through the 'Vagabond Club Round Robin' until the 1960s.

Similarly, his more specifically academic interests ranged well beyond the limits of theology; indeed he always remained acutely aware of the limits of that particular subject. He paid tribute specifically to his professors in philosophy and literature. (Given his propensity to self-criticism, his later confession to not having worked hard enough is rather suspect.) Novels became an abiding source of refreshment; in his eighties he wrote:

> *In the last few years I have read through all Scott's novels, all of George Eliot's and Thackeray's. I punctuate with a modern novel or an old favourite like Trollope. I am now wallowing in Charles Dickens, although he is an acquired taste, like cricket, for a Scot.*[5]

Poetry became a source of truth and enlightenment. Kay Fenn, an SCM staff colleague in the 1930s, claimed that Robert could say more by reading a poem than had been said in the previous two hours discussion.[6]

After graduation, and his ordination in his father's little church in Bothwell, one of Robert's first tasks as Scottish Secretary in 1925 was to chair the Manchester Quadrennial, the latest in a series of large student gatherings started in Liverpool in 1896, followed by London in 1900, Edinburgh in 1904, Liverpool in 1908 and 1912, and Glasgow in 1921. The theme was 'The World Task of the Christian Church'. There was a typical attendance of around 2000 from British Universities and, in addition, many overseas delegations; there were usually over 25 or more nationalities present at any major British SCM conference. The impact of speakers such as T Z Koo on China and J H Oldham on 'Race' was developed further in group discussion in the context of common worship. One of the results of this Quadrennial and the subsequent tour by T Z Koo round the universities, was further to bridge what gulf remained between the 'internationalist' and the 'foreign mission' approach: 'missions' were now seen as 'Christian international co-operation'.

An indication of this on Robert's home ground was the opening of the International House in Glasgow in October 1925 under the joint auspices of the YMCA and the SCM. In addition, there was a re-emphasis on the part played by economic exploitation in the maintenance of injustice at home and abroad – a factor widely appreciated at least in SCM circles since William Temple's contribution to the Liverpool Quadrennial in 1912; this had stimulated an awareness of Christian involvement in collective as well as individual guilt.

Suzanne de Dietrich, later a close friend and colleague in the WSCF, writes in her *Cinquante Ans d'Histoire*:

The British SCM played a unique role in the annals of the Federation. The Swanwick Conferences and the 'Quadrennials' were always open to students from the European Continent as well as those from Africa and Asia; and it was there that many men and women of all races discovered the Federation. Whether it concerned apologetics, biblical studies, missions to the Universities or overseas missions; whether it raised

social questions from the practical angle of the Settlements or the
theoretical angle in conferences and study groups, or both at the same time
in the industrial and rural departments, the SCM broke new ground.
By the outreach of its congresses, by the publications of the SCM Press,
it exerted a vast influence not only on the English public, but in all
countries where English was spoken or read.[7]

Quadrennials were, however, rare high points, and the day-to-day work of an SCM Secretary in Scotland was in many ways exceedingly humdrum and, superficially at least, unrewarding. It involved visiting, supporting, sometimes starting, student groups in universities and colleges throughout Scotland. As Leslie Hunter, then Study Secretary, later the distinguished Bishop of Sheffield, wrote in his 1920 report, 'we represent a constituency which has continually to start again from the beginning with each student generation'.[8]

For this reason, it was the tradition of the SCM that initiation of policy and programme should lie with students themselves – both locally and at national level; a Scottish Council including representatives from every branch met annually, as did the British General Committee. Staff Secretaries were in an advisory capacity, and the amount of advice given and accepted depended largely on the personal relationships developed between the individual Secretary and the different student leaders.

Some specifically Scottish problems had emerged from the reports of the local staff in 1923 and 1924: J W D Smith[9] complains that 'finances are haphazard … appeals unco-ordinated … "Senior Friends" alienated.'[10] Dorothy Steven stressed the need for 'a senior man with pastoral gifts who would make himself trusted by the Church', and she writes of the Edinburgh situation: 'the men have a deeply-rooted habit of talking fervently about fellowship and scrapping like tigers when they aren't talking about it, and the women regard the men with the tolerant contempt of more reasonable creatures.'[11]

Typically, Robert's approach was fundamentally positive: 'there is a new spirit in the Scottish Universities', and in Edinburgh there is 'plenty of religious interest in the University at large', although this is not well served by 'a strain of narrower piety in the meetings' combined with 'timidity on University issues and ... religiously intensive lack of commonsense planning'. In Glasgow he finds 'a youthfulness and gaiety of spirit and a quite definite if sporadic sense of responsibility'. Of the Dundee group he comments wryly, 'they are largely disillusioned churchridden folk!' A month after his appointment in September 1925 he wrote that the Edinburgh students, although friendly, didn't 'actually invite me to things', but within weeks he can add, 'I may be making many mistakes, but I am glad to say that we parted better friends than when we met'.[12]

For a fair understanding of Robert's character it is essential to realise that for him friendship was of the nature of the Gospel itself; it was never merely the means to an end, such as the conversion of individuals or the smooth-running of an organisation. Dorothy wrote of him at this period: 'You ... are near the men and women you come among'[13]; and later, 'you ... who are so busy at the task of friendship'.[14]

Yet in the commonplace books he occasionally kept during holiday breaks in the 1920s and 30s, he continually criticises himself for not caring enough for others: 'the difficult thing is to go on trying the way of fellowship.' 'Christian love,' he writes, 'meant having that inside knowledge of what life felt like to others.'[15] Sometimes the internal evidence of his own musings testifies to a success he did not recognise: 'General Committee ran for three days. The difficult questions were staff and finance. At first I thought it was a hopeless committee, but later on it grew into a fellowship.'[16] Robert was in the chair.

There is no doubt that the most significant event of 1926 for Robert was his marriage to Dorothy Steven, his predecessor as leader of the Scottish SCM staff team. Four years older, she had pursued a brilliant student career, first at Edinburgh, gaining first class honours in classics and a 'Ferguson' scholarship – the first woman to do so; this took her to Cambridge after a year's Assistantship in the Humanities Department in Aberdeen. At Newnham she changed her initial Classics to English, emerging with another first class honours and as Senior Student of the college.

A keen sense of Christian vocation, the undoubted discrimination against women in the academic world, a growing preference for education seen as the personal development of the individual rather than as the pursuit of a specific discipline, led her away from an academic career and to accept the job of Missionary Study Secretary of the SCM based at Annandale, the London headquarters of the Movement, where R O Hall was her male colleague. This, followed by her work in Scotland and marriage to Robert, ended her father's 'old man's dream' of her future as the first woman professor of classics, or even as head of 'Trinity or St John's'! [17]

Reserved, intellectual, perceptive, seeing herself as 'socially ... hopeless', [18] Dorothy was so surprised at Robert's proposal that she rang him up the same evening to ask if he really meant it! Outsiders, then and later, saw them as an unlikely match. The letters between them, however, from the Indian expedition onwards, disclose a most genuine and developing meeting of minds. They shared a profound Christian commitment and sense of vocation, a love of Scotland and an enjoyment of literature. The difference in temperament, the source of some preliminary difficulty, brought them in the end to a complementary marriage of the greatest strength and support to both. In the early years of the Second World War, when they were often apart, Dorothy wrote:

> *There is so much to thank God for. So very much. To have tested each other and found – not that the other is perfect but that he or she is just what we need and value most – surely that is something of the secret of happy marriage.* [19]

> *All these years of adjustment, when you had so much to put up with and were so forbearing and good to me, have made our inheritance so much the richer now ... our love was so deeply grounded that we could go through difficult adjustments due to our peculiar and diverse psychological backgrounds.* [20]

During the next thirty years Robert's work was to take them from Edinburgh to London, from London to Geneva, from Geneva to Toronto and back to Geneva, and finally to Scotland. Some people then – and perhaps even more now – would welcome such variety, but, for all the valiant insistence on its positive aspects which emerges from their letters, it is plain that both found something unnatural in such a life. It was seen, however, as a necessary cost of discipleship.

Robert was clear that the price was paid most dearly by his wife: 'I go away to meet new people: she stays lonely at home.'[21] It remains more difficult to reroot home *and* child – Steven was born in 1927 – than to tackle a new job. Dorothy had plenty of inner resources, but not a quick and easy facility for making new friends. Even one generation later it is likely that a woman of her abilities would have pursued more individual activities of her own, but there is no indication in her letters that she resented in any way the supportive role she had assumed. She remained constantly concerned about the pressures on Robert and about the upbringing of Steven and showed little concern for herself. It remained for Robert to regret that she was insufficiently valued for herself and her abilities, and to carry with him an ill-defined sense of guilt on the subject. Scots are – or were – frequently undemonstrative in family life, and a puzzled American colleague wondered that Robert occasionally addressed his wife as 'woman', unaware that this is a term of affection in the Scottish vernacular.[22]

Through Dorothy he came to another relationship which he greatly valued – with his father-in-law, Dr George Steven, minister of St Bernard's United Free Church in Stockbridge, Edinburgh. This remarkable man, respected in ecclesiastical circles throughout Britain, had 'earned his way ... as a pupil teacher' to university and the ministry in the classic Scottish pattern. With 'all the instincts and habits of a scholar', he became known for the breadth of his churchmanship and the prescience of his vision.

Dr Steven was an extraordinarily early pioneer in the critical appreciation of the part psychology might play in pastoral theology and practice, giving the Cunningham Lectures at New College in 1911 on 'The Psychology of the Christian Soul'. Although eighty years old when Robert met him in 1925, he became a loved mentor and friend until his death in 1930. Robert wrote of him:

> *He was always a radical in his approach to Christian truth. I remember helping him to pack a bag of books for a holiday in Deeside. As I put*

*in a whole series of lives of Christ I asked him if this exercise was
necessary! He said, 'I have recently begun to revise many of my earlier
ideas about Jesus and I cannot rest until I have studied and reflected
further'. Then he added with unaffected simplicity, 'Of course I shall
see him soon and I shall know'. With an 'astonishingly catholic view
of the Church', he had gathered 'a fine library of Christian mysticism'
and treasured 'two crucifixes on his walls given him by Roman Catholic
friends'.*[23]

In the course of his wise and witty correspondence with Dorothy
when she was homesick at Cambridge, George Steven wrote,
with greater relevance than he knew to her future life:

*Homesickness is not only an aching for something you have lost for a
time but for something towards which you are pressing out to attain.
When you have realised this you get your old home back again in a
richer way. The home you recover is in the heart not a place but a
spirit.*[24]

Notes to Chapter 4

1   Letter from Tissington Tatlow to Dr Macgregor, 5.1.1924: SCM
     Archives, Selly Oak Colleges' Library, Birmingham.
2   Letter from Tissington Tatlow to Robert, 22.12.1924: ibid.
3   Letter from Robert to Dorothy, early 1925: Mackie Papers, Edin-
     burgh.
4   'One man's experience of the SCM', 1982: ibid.
5   'Pleasure in Old Age', 1982: ibid.
6   Interview with Eric and Kay Fenn, July 1991.
7   *Cinquante Ans d'Histoire,* Suzanne de Dietrich (translation by Jean
     Fraser).
8   SCM Archives.
9   Later on the staff of Jordanhill Training College, Glasgow.
10   SCM Archives.
11   Report from Dorothy Steven, 8.10.1923: ibid.
12   Reports from Robert, 1925/1926: ibid.
13   Letter from Dorothy to Robert, January 1929: Mackie Papers.

14   Letter from Dorothy to Robert, 21.7.1936: ibid.
15   Commonplace books, 1933: ibid.
16   Ibid.
17   Letter from George Steven to Dorothy, 17.8.1918: Mackie Papers.
18   Letter from Dorothy to Robert, 21.7.1935: ibid.
19   Letter from Dorothy to Robert, 14.12.1949: ibid.
20   Letter from Dorothy to Robert, 30.11.1945: ibid.
21   Commonplace books, 22.8.1933: ibid.
22   Interview with Marie-Jeanne Coleman, July 1991.
23   Letter from Robert to grandsons: Mackie papers.
24   Letter from George Steven to Dorothy, 19.8.1918: ibid.

CHAPTER 5

The Scottish Base

TISSINGTON Tatlow had written in 1924 that in his experience 'good national secretaries will be rotten financiers'[1], but Robert proved to be the exception. Indeed, he was in general to develop the self-discipline, where he felt circumstances required it, to give priority to those aspects of his work which least suited his predelictions This became a trait which was to distinguish him throughout his career. Any other attitude he saw as self-indulgent.

He regularly organised and spoke at meetings of senior people in the business world, and here his family and university connections proved useful. He was already known and respected for his leadership in summer camps by such bodies as the YMCA and the Scottish Schoolboys' Clubs. His readiness to speak to church leaders and others about the SCM, and his good-humoured response to criticism, helped in the course of time to dissipate distrust. He wrote:

> *On the whole in Scotland the SCM is viewed suspiciously by the churches .... There is a feeling that the SCM is not doing its job, which is partly founded in fact, and partly on a misapprehension as to our job .... It is difficult to remedy this save by becoming friendly with more ministers. Denominational and congregational consciousness seems very strong. We are either unnecessary in the minds of many, or else a rather extravagant and independent show, which they are not sure of.*[2]

A great deal of his time was taken up attempting to heal in Scotland, as later on a wider stage, a deeply damaging rift in the original Student Christian Movement. This had begun in pre-war Cambridge and took final organisational form in the foundation in

1928 of the Inter-Varsity Fellowship (IVF). Although in different places and on different occasions, particular circumstances and the clash of particular personalities provided immediate reasons for conflict and the setting up of alternative Christian groups, over the years there were two main causes for the division: one theological and one organisational.

First of all, the SCM regarded itself as the servant of the churches in the world of higher education, not as a church in itself: it was thought inappropriate, therefore, for it to set doctrinal tests, and the condition of membership was defined accordingly:

> *The Student Christian Movement is a fellowship of students who desire to understand the Christian faith and live the Christian life. This desire is the only condition of membership.*[3]

Doctrinal tests were the business of churches, affecting individuals when they wished to join a church. This attitude on the part of the SCM led to inclusiveness rather than exclusiveness, not only regarding membership, but also in the choice both of programmes and speakers.

In contrast, the IVF affirmed a specific doctrinal basis, related to a particular theology of the atonement. Subscription to this was mandatory for all members, who were sometimes required to sign the relevant statement annually. As Douglas Johnson explains in his history of the IVF, *Contending for the Faith* (Inter-Varsity Press), this position demanded that invitations to speakers at all events should be restricted to those who were in full accordance with the 'fundamental truths' set out in the constitution. Branches were quite explicitly forbidden to co-operate with any other religious group which did not adhere to the same basis.

There were certainly often those within the SCM who themselves were sympathetic to the theology of the IVF: the disagreement was over the claim to exclusive truth and the ban on co-operation. To the SCM, disunity amongst Christians was a scandal, an obstacle to the preaching of a Gospel of reconciliation which declared 'that all may be one'.[4]

The second issue concerned the less democratic nature of the IVF organisation where doctrinal consistency was ensured by a greater centralisation of authority. So foreign was such a structure to normal student life that, more than once, SCM headquarters staff were asked by the IVF, in Christian charity, to persuade their local SCM branches to stop suggesting co-operation in prayer, Bible study and missionary campaigns. Staff appreciated the dilemma – and also the irony!

The plethora of Christian groups in universities and colleges in the 1920s must have given rise to a negative reaction in many – 'a plague o' both your houses!' Robert himself, by background, temperament, training and conviction, could never have been described as anything but an 'evangelical' in the widest sense of that much abused word. Consequently, where some were appalled and others irritated by the persistence of the schism, he was then, and always remained, deeply hurt by the attitude of the IVF, even though he understood it. He could, however, never accept that one theological interpretation, a minority view within the broad range of historic Christian orthodoxy, could encompass the 'final truth' of the Gospel; rather, he found within that Gospel an imperative to recognise and affirm all those who wished to respond.

He was convinced that the SCM must have room for the great variety of theological and ecclesiological positions, indeed that it was the poorer when any excluded themselves. As an example, in Edinburgh University in 1928, where existed the SCM, the Christian Union (IVF), the Evangelical Alliance, the Edinburgh Colleges' Evangelical Union (for running campaigns), and several denominational societies, he encouraged a joint co-ordinating committee. When that failed, he tried simple friendship.

His attitude is well expressed in his reference to an approach for help from a group at the College of Art. 'The leader,' he writes, 'was a confirmed atheist and the discussion very radical, but there is life, and frankness. It is a magnificent opportunity.'[5] In contrast, Lloyd Jones, popular preacher and long a senior adviser with the IVF, used to say: 'As a missionary I do not discuss, I proclaim.'[6]

In the context of post-war unemployment and seriously sub-standard housing, Robert encouraged growing student concern with social issues. He commented approvingly on 'more heart-searching amongst men in Glasgow than in the other centres at the time of the Strike .... In a time like this the setting of a great city is very helpful'. [7]

Attitudes of SCM students seem to have been very different from the image in popular myth of the student as strike-breaker, although the myth itself may have only an Oxbridge reference. Support was willingly given to European Student Relief, founded by the World's Student Christian Federation in 1920 in response to the acute material, intellectual and spiritual needs of students and professors in the destructive aftermath of war; until then there had been no distinctive relief agency for the universities.

As important as the aid itself, was the method of delivery, which had to include the elements of reconciliation and respect. From the first, help was given irrespective of religion or nationality, and it was decided in 1925 to start the International Student Service (ISS) to provide a neutral base leading to even broader cooperation. The various national SCMs, however, remained the main source of local support, all the stronger in Scotland because the Director of European Student Relief in Vienna and Russia was Donald Grant, who had been Scottish SCM Secretary during the war, part of which he had spent in Dartmoor prison because of his pacifist convictions.

In the 1920s Robert was not alone in stressing the significance of the lay vocation for the Christian; that other great ecumenical Scot, J H Oldham, was to prove himself both prophet and radical pioneer in this regard, although too little heeded. With the increasing secularisation of society it was becoming clear that 'mission' or outreach had to be seen in terms of the Christian in his daily work, as trade unionist or employer, teacher or student, doctor, factory worker, artist or housewife. The SCM's emphasis on the demands of the student vocation, perceived as the search for truth in community, gave several generations an experience which disabused them of the notion that 'ordination to word and sacrament' was in some way a higher calling. The churches of the Reformation, however, which were dominant in Scotland, frequently laboured under the misapprehension that the matter was satisfactorily subsumed under the institution of the eldership. Dr Elisabeth Hewat wrote at the time: 'The church has developed an ecclesiastical laity which is divorced from the ordinary man.' [8]

Also in the spirit of the times, and with a strong personal commitment to 'the removal of false barriers between men and women'[9], Robert was able to do away with the traditional organisational separation into men's and women's groups at local level of the SCM. It was, in the British church context, to be within the ranks of the SCM that a natural and productive partnership between men and women, without confrontation or explicit ideology, was first developed. This sat easily with most types of the theology of ministry in the Reformed tradition, where initial resistance to women's ordination mostly sprang from social conservatism. The exception was, of course, where Biblical literalism held sway.

For other SCM members, in this instance mainly Anglicans, there were frequently painful encounters with rigid ecclesiastical structures when university years were over. The nineteenth century era of worldwide missionary expansion happened to have occurred at the same time as the emergence of the women's movement in its earliest forms. Consequently, more by coincidence than intent, 'overseas mission' had provided an arena for the abilities and initiative of many women to whom their own churches and societies offered little opportunity. Ruth Rouse, in her history of the first thirty years of the World's Student Christian Federation (WSCF), reveals how its origin lies more properly with Grace Wilder and the women of the Mount Holyoke Missionary Association started in 1878, than with her brother, Robert, and the more famous Princeton men of the Student Volunteer Movement founded at Mount Hermon in 1886.[10]

By 1913 women members of the ruling General Committee of the WSCF included those from India, Ceylon, South Africa and Japan. It is unfortunate that, as the ecumenical movement has become church-based in the second half of the century (a necessary development in itself if it is to achieve its unifying purpose), this natural contribution of women to its leadership has been largely lost. It is a price which has had to be paid for the greater involvement of first the Orthodox, and then the Roman tradition, on all other grounds to be welcomed without reserve.

In the Glasgow of 1927, ecumenical advance was achieved by obtaining the co-operation of Roman Catholics in a 'Religion and Life Week', in which Archie Craig[11] was a principal speaker. Robert's own appreciation of differing traditions of worship was enhanced by his friendship with Herbert Kelly, leader of the Kelham Fathers, Society of St John the Evangelist, an Anglo-Catholic missionary order:

> ... it was the sense of concreteness in a liturgical approach, separate from feeling or opinion that appealed to me .... I did not at all mind being excluded from Communion, because I was fascinated by the tremendous sincerity of belief which made men exclude me.[12]

It would be good if such an attitude could still obtain in some instances of present eucharistic separation. Locally, however, he found, as many have since, that the introduction of devotional 'quiet days' was frequently difficult in presbyterian Scotland.

In his Annual Report for 1927, Robert quoted Randall Davidson, then Archbishop of Canterbury, who commended the SCM in a charge to his archdiocese in these terms:

> Organisation is too rigid and prosaic a word to describe a movement which in its spontaneity and buoyancy, its international character and its quiet force seems to me one of the most remarkable movements which any part of Christendom at any place or time has seen.

'Such a verdict,' Robert himself comments, 'at once humbles and encourages those to whom for a space is given the direction of the Movement's affairs.'[13]

Such a perspective, however, goes some way to explain why, after some hesitation, he agreed to join the London General Secretariat in 1929. Dorothy was doubtful:

> I feel as if I could scarcely bear you to go on longer with the SCM – You are not detached enough, perhaps, to stand continuously such a knock-about life .... One thing I am going to insist on is that you are not to let yourself get so tired and so worried as you have done. You have to take times of leisure – happy leisure.[14]

Robert had indeed quite often recorded that he was 'hopelessly tired' and, characteristically, once added, 'resolved ... not to think myself virtuous in getting tired'! After one particularly wearing conference he had indigestion for a week and dreaded the start of the autumn term. To his own cost he had started to earn his reputation for 'saving the day' at difficult or contentious meetings or ill-organised conferences; students must after all, by definition, remain permanent amateurs at organisation, and so the need for such intervention was not infrequent.

> *The way in which you pulled the whole thing together, saving what could be saved from the previous three nights, and giving folk something to take away as a permanent possession, could hardly have been improved.*[15]

As the years went by this reputation, enhanced by the increasing significance of the occasions, must have become something of a burden: that of an ecumenical troubleshooter called on when the situation was too hot for anyone else to handle, whether at the first World Council of Churches Assembly in Amsterdam or in the process of attempting to unify congregations in the Scotland of the 1960s.

As Robert left Edinburgh for the south he recorded a series of resolutions in his commonplace book:

> <u>Discipline</u>: *We think of discipline as dealing only with difficult or disagreeable things. It also has to deal with pleasant things. Just as important as forcing oneself to study or to pray is making up one's mind to take leisure,*
> > *to read novels,*
> > *to play with Steven,*
> > *to play with Dorothy,*
> > *to read together.*
> *The real basis of work of a family man should be his family – not his office.*

Again:

> *God is Love.*
> 1   *A loving purpose for the world.*
> 2   *A loving experience in my own life.*

3   A loving relationship with men and women.

The SCM is a gift of Love
to pass this knowledge from one generation of students to another
1   By life
2   By speech
3   By opportunities of understanding and service.[16]

In 1929 the United Free Church of Scotland (in which Robert had been brought up) and the Church of Scotland were reunited. To his delight, he was asked to represent the SCM at the celebrations in Edinburgh. As the product of this satisfactory and, for most of his generation at least, relatively painless process of church reunion, Robert could indeed be described as a 'natural' ecumenist. Reporting at the time he wrote:

I stayed with one who was at college with Henry Drummond[17] *and Robert Louis Stevenson, and who has grown old in the service of the Church; something of his deep conviction of the worth of the events which he had lived to see seized hold of me, and it was with an expectant heart that I went out into the streets to see the Union.*

'Into the streets' – for the really important things still happen in the streets of Edinburgh where everyone can see. I stood opposite the house in which Burns once lived in the Lawnmarket, and every window of those high, romantic slums had faces in it. We were all waiting for 'the processions'. Slowly, almost silently, with no pomp and circumstance, they came. The 'Auld Kirk' came down the Lawnmarket, and the 'U.F.' came up the from the Mound. They were long columns of black coated ministers and elders – old men who had known the bitterness of religious controversy in Scotland, and young men who had been at Swanwick or Moffat[18] *a year or two ago. In a high wind, for Edinburgh did its characteristic best for the occasion, the two columns met in the High Street and marched on four abreast to the High Kirk. As Moderator bowed and shook hands with Moderator, as minister and elder greeted the men whom chance had brought along the street to be their companions, the crowd began to sing. There in that place which has seen most of Scotland's history, often a sad history, where men have marched singing to their death for conscience' sake, the words and notes of the old*

psalms hung lingeringly among the crow-stepped gables, and passed up into the windy sky above the crown of St Giles.

Later in the day twelve thousand men and women gathered in the Hall of Assembly to witness the signing of the Act of Union ....

He finishes with the words of the visiting Archbishop of Canterbury (Randall Davidson):

The man must be dull of spirit, and feeble of fibre whose pulse is not quickened as he looks round this great Assembly.[19]

In his address to the reunited Assembly on this occasion Robert concluded:

This great act of union will encourage and inspire the Student Christian Movement, and the prayer of its members is that God may greatly bless the Church of Scotland for the Christian good of the land, and especially of her four ancient universities and many colleges.[20]

The Church of Scotland's letter of thanks for many years decorated the walls of the London headquarters of the SCM at Annandale.

Notes to Chapter 5

1   Letter from Tissington Tatlow, 3.11.1924: SCM Archives, Selly Oak Colleges' Library, Birmingham.
2   Report by Robert from Scotland, June 1927: ibid.
3   'The Aim and Basis of the SCM': ibid.
4   John's Gospel, 17:21.
5   Report by Robert, December 1926: SCM Archives.
6   Recorded as late as March 1950 in the official discussions between the SCM and the IVF: ibid.
7   Report by Robert, Autumn 1925: ibid.
8   SCM Archives.
9   Report by Robert, Autumn 1925: ibid.
10 Chapter 1, *The World's Student Christian Federation*, Ruth Rouse: SCM Press.

11 Later first General Secretary of the British Council of Churches and subsequently Chaplain to Glasgow University and a Moderator of the General Assembly of the Church of Scotland.

12 'On Growing up in the Church', undated manuscript: Mackie Papers, Edinburgh.

13 SCM Archives.

14 Letter from Dorothy to Robert, September 1928: Mackie Papers.

15 Letter from K T Witz, last secretary to Tissington Tatlow and interview, July 1991: ibid.

16 Mackie Papers.

17 Professor Henry Drummond was the outstanding progenitor of the SCM amongst Scottish students in the last decades of the nineteenth century.

18 British and Scottish SCM conference centres.

19 Letter from Robert published in *The Student Movement* October 1929.

20 SCM Archives.

CHAPTER 6

The British Dimension

IT is not unusual for problems to arise in any organisation when a leader of outstanding talent finally gives way to a successor. By 1929 Tissington Tatlow had served on the staff of the SCM for 29 years, all but one as General Secretary. During this period he had acquired many colleagues of considerable distinction, but normally they served for a few years only, then moved on to positions of leadership in church or society.[1]

Tissington Tatlow, on the other hand, had made the SCM his whole life, and achieved for it a position of respect and some influence within both the churches and higher education. With roots in the 'evangelical' wing of the Church of Ireland, he had evolved into a 'high' Anglican as the result of his ecumenical experience. He had provided what he called 'the permanent element', the continuity, the point of reference and, eventually, the father figure, as the gap between his age and that of the generality of staff widened to between twenty and thirty years. For the last 25 years, he had retained the same chief assistant, Zoe Fairfield. Without the particular difficulties arising from the war, he might have left earlier, but, in any case, when the succession came into question in 1927, he found it scarcely possible to envisage the Movement without him.

A main concern on his part was the SCM's standing with the Church of England. The relationship between the Church of England and the Church of Scotland, two 'national' churches, has never been less than amicable during this century, each tending to leave the other to its own devices. Occasionally, however, circumstances of geography, history and hierarchical thinking (ecclesiological and sociological), have led to an element of

English myopia in their association. So it was that initially 'T' (as he was commonly known), felt it necessary that he be replaced by a 'senior Anglican'.

He proposed that he himself should move to a new full-time position as non-executive 'Chairman' of the SCM and Editor of *The Student Movement*, providing oversight to a secretariat of three, with the addition of an experienced office administrator. One of the team of three should be Secretary to the General Committee of the SCM and as such be in some sense *primus inter pares* – first among equals. The proposal proceeded through all the correct constitutional mechanisms but T's hand, and indeed fears, are obvious.

Not too surprisingly to the onlooker, a letter of invitation on these lines was declined by the 'senior Anglican' – John Maud, a layman later to achieve prominence as a distinguished civil servant. It took someone of Robert's modesty and humour to accept such a role when his name emerged as the unanimous choice in the next round of consultations. Only his particular combination of conciliatory talents could have accomplished the transition so that by 1933 he was acknowledged leader and General Secretary, albeit with a quite different management style. Tissington Tatlow meanwhile withdrew happily to an entirely 'Honorary Chaplain' status, a status he retained until his death in 1957.[2]

The situation was eased by the fact that Robert could genuinely appreciate and respect difference, an attitude rarer than we think (probably because most of us erroneously imagine that we possess it). His regard for his predecessor remained with him always. In 1933 he wrote to him in the following terms:

> *I sometimes wonder how you bore with a generation which had little sense of history* .... *I should imagine we shall find that nothing really new was invented after the war in the Movement* .... [Tatlow was writing his history of the SCM at the time] .... *I remember that we were often irritated with your references back 'over a long period of years', but I do not ever remember your losing patience with us. 'Why won't people allow the Movement to make mistakes?' you said.*[3]

Long afterwards in 1954 at Evanston, when Robert was

assisting in the organisation of the World Council of Churches' second Assembly, he was so conscious of emulating the other man's methods that more than once he absentmindedly addressed a colleague as 'T'. Nevertheless, when his own time came to leave in 1938, he was determined to make the process easier and more satisfactory for his successor, 'Billy' Greer[4]: 'I succeeded a magnificent administrator of the "keep everything in your own hands" type.'[5]

Robert, Dorothy and Steven moved to London with rather more stoicism than enthusiasm, but this is not an uncommon Scots reaction to such a circumstance then or now. Returning from Edinburgh a few years later, he wrote 'and so back I come from a city, which is a city, to this strange labyrinth in which I live in exile'.[6] Yet in another and very real sense, Robert was 'at home' anywhere through his capacity to be 'host' to others wherever he was.

Events in the 1930s were dominated by economic depression and related political responses – the rise of fascism and communism. British students in general shared a legacy of anti-war feeling derived from the tragedy of 1914–1918 and the perception of a bungled peace settlement. At home there was the phenomenon of mass unemployment and its associated miseries. Reactions took many forms: a few were extreme, from individual participation in the Spanish Civil War to secret service work on behalf of the USSR. Hindsight is, indeed, a constant temptation as we reiterate the successive events: Japan's invasion of Manchuria in 1932; Nazi dominance in Germany and Hitler's successful interventions in the Rhineland, Austria and Czechoslovakia.

It is impossible, however, to read of the attempts of the British SCM to bring a contemporary Christian perspective to bear without both sympathy and respect. Davis McCaughey's excellent account, in his *Christian Obedience in the University* (1930–1950)[7], is full of insight and is indeed required reading for anyone with an interest in twentieth century church history. A very specific understanding and sensitivity arose from the SCM's commitment to the Student Christian Movements in so many other countries through that 'work of God'[8] – the World Student Christian Federation. Two examples must suffice: in 1930, in response to the struggle for independence in India, Robert wrote from the British to the Indian SCM a letter of solidarity; the next year an appeal from the Inter-collegiate Christian Union in Shanghai, sent within days of the Manchurian invasion in September, elicited an immediate cable from the British General Committee to both Japan and China:

> *Deeply sympathize with difficulties Christian men and women students China Japan. Recognize Western responsibility common failure build forces for peace. Still working praying Christian solution.*

One of the few achievements in which Robert later took a justifiable pride was his transformation of the existing annual 'Finance Week' into 'Federation Week', giving it a wider and more imaginative scope. It has been said that 'he internationalised the SCM in an international time'.

When Robert estimated that his own views on international affairs in the 1920s had been characterised by unrealistic idealism, he spoke for a whole generation which had pinned its hopes to the League of Nations. But realist and idealist were united, at least in Britain, in support of the World Disarmament Conference in 1932. Disillusionment with that occasion was reported by the new General Secretary of the WSCF – Visser 't Hooft – in these terms:

> *The outstanding impression of the Conference is that there is little real discussion in the sense of facing the situation of others and of taking each other seriously. It might be said that the whole Conference is a series of monologues!*[9]

The subsequent failure of the League to acquire power to control aggression in the Far East or in Europe led to a multi-plicity of conscientiously held views within and between differ-ent national SCMs. The arguments were rarely theoretical for long, as they were undertaken by the very generation which found itself obliged to respond by action when war struck. As General Secretary, Robert was called upon to 'hold the ring' for pacifist and non-pacifist, for Marxist and anti-communist, for those who saw disarmament or those who saw rearmament as the way to peace. The complex, thoughtful character of General

Committee memoranda, study materials, reading lists and conference programmes bear witness to the breadth and depth of this
mediating function.[10] In many ways Robert was admirably suited
by temperament for the task; he found it easier to enter into the
feelings of others and to appreciate the strength of their convictions
than to convince himself that any one position was absolute for
him.

One of the necessary gifts for such a time was the capacity to
recognise the need for a new agenda, to discover and present to a
student generation those who had prophetic insight into the situation. The list of participants at various events is a fascinating
one: it includes C F Andrews, Donald and John Baillie, Dietrich
Bonhoeffer, Cecil of Chelwood, T S Eliot, C S Lewis, Donald
Mackinnon, Reinhold Niebuhr, John Macmurray, Karl Mannheim,
Middleton Murry, Michael Polanyi, Dorothy Sayers, William
Temple. Davis McCaughey singles out the Edinburgh Quadrennial
of 1933:

> *It is questionable whether through all their many services to the British*
> *SCM, Robert Mackie and Eric Fenn ever did anything more influential*
> *in the student field than in the devising of this conference, planning its*
> *programme, coaching the speakers, training the leaders, preparing the*
> *branches for its reception and following up its impact. Edinburgh 1933*
> *announced in no uncertain terms that the old world of adjustment*
> *was dead and that a new era of reassessment, of investigation of the*
> *profoundest questions of human existence within history and in the*
> *context of eternity, had dawned.*[11]

The most significant speakers were Hanns Lilje[12] from the
German SCM (who brought a delegation of around 25 with him)
on 'Christian Community and Communism', and J H Oldham on
'Faith in God and faith in man'. Some senior friends expressed a
fear that the 'overseas mission' emphasis had lost its place, but
the change was rather one of perspective; in Robert's words,
missionaries now went 'not as fathers but as brothers and friends'.[13]

The material conditions of students in many countries worsened.
The International Student Service, 'springing out of the Federation
and of the same family', reported in 1933 that virtually half the

graduates of the German higher education system were unemployed; from 1933 Nazi repression produced a regular flow of academic refugees and by 1937 Chinese students were in desperate straits. Robert became Treasurer of the WSCF and took a direct lead in the SCM's co-operation with the ISS both in Britain and abroad. McCaughey writes:

> ... *the movement was fortunate to have men who could interpret, as Robert Mackie did, the abiding Christian duty of compassion and evangelism in the new world of strife and terror.*[14]

His proactive role in the area of student relief in this period was, of course, only the forerunner of his increasing involvement during and after the Second World War. Now, as an officer of the Federation, he frequently attended meetings on the continent, and spent two months in North America in 1936, building up a thorough knowledge of its world network. His notebooks are full of the thoughts of leaders such as T Z Koo from China and Reinhold von Thadden from Germany. These Federation links, Eric Fenn's and Lesslie Newbigin's[15] intimate concern, along with interest in the theology of Karl Barth, all helped to ensure that in Britain the greatest sensitivity to the situation of the German churches from which the phenomenon of the Confessing Church emerged was to be found in ecumenical circles, in which at this time the SCM played so significant a part.

This sympathy, however, arose more from personal human concern rather than much genuine understanding of the nature of the Confessing Church and its theological and political attitudes. Robert's listening silence was perhaps a more appropriate response than he knew.

As General Secretary, Robert saw his own role essentially in terms of helping others to gain the experience and skills for future leadership. This meant that he frequently sent them to conferences and consultations rather than himself. An instance of this occurred at the 1937 Oxford Conference on Church, Community and State, when many of the overseas participants who were looking forward to to meeting him were surprised to discover that he had stayed at Annandale to keep the routine work going. He had a fine sense of how to select the appropriate person for the specific occasion or job and a particular gift for raising their enthusiasm. Eric Duncan, a colleague both in Britain and Geneva, recalls being interviewed by him in 1935 in the middle of a hectic Swanwick conference for the post of Edinburgh International Secretary. With total concentration, Robert 'poured out' everything he knew and felt about the situation, the problems, the people, the possibilities: 'He didn't try to dictate the job to me' Eric Duncan remembers. 'He just made it easy ... he was just someone who was greatly concerned about me and that I should succeed ... it was a tremendous experience.' [16]

Perhaps the most striking example of Robert's enabling function on the domestic front was his encouragement and consistent support of the Industrial Department. This was a largely new initiative arising in response to economic decline, unemployment, hunger marches, technological change and the different kind of education available in technical colleges and departments. The initiative was shared with the Auxiliary Movement, an organisation of lay graduates who had generally come through the SCM in their student days and who, in this instance, were working in industry or commerce. By 1936, when its activities were assessed for input into the 1937 Oxford Conference, the Industrial Department had held two National and one International Conference in 1932, 1934, and 1935. Add to this fifty local conferences, workcamps (one to build a playground for miners' children), projects, action committees, variously including employers, trade unions, the unemployed, economists, farmers, technical students, theologians – and the scope of the enterprise begins to become clear.

The moving spirit and 'ideas man' was Edwin Barker, the SCM Industrial Secretary, but little could have been accomplished without Robert's personal commitment and promotion. Indeed, he saw the relationship of the Student Industrial Committee to the SCM General Committee as possibly becoming very similar, in terms of the Christian vocation of the individual, to that of the Student Volunteer Movement in earlier days.

Less surprisingly, perhaps, given his general theological background, he embraced with enthusiasm the resurgence in the 1930s of Bible study of a new depth and urgency, assisted in Britain by the writings of C H Dodd and on the continent by the guidance of Suzanne de Dietrich.[17] It is regrettable that the pioneering work of the SCM in group Bible study methods, mediating to the laity the insights of a century of Biblical scholarship, should have been followed so slowly by the churches at large. Only such a rigorous and inspiriting approach can break the bonds of literalism and re-establish the proper authority of the Bible.

Robert welcomed unreservedly the progress in ecumenical relationships which was leading towards the establishment of a World Council of Churches; as an officer of the WSCF and a member of its European Council his own ecumenical experience had broadened and deepened. He saw the SCM as having a crucial educative role in leading students to face the scandal of division between the denominations, learning how to maintain a critical loyalty within one tradition, whilst at the same time being sensitive to diversity in doctrine and liturgy within and between others. He really did try very hard to practise what he preached in these matters, but was never allowed to forget the occasion at a staff 'retreat' when he was discovered standing on his head at the bottom of the garden as a relief from what he had found to be an undue time on his knees![18]

He was deeply interested in furthering the participation of the Orthodox world within the Federation: the Russian SCM had joined in 1913, and, although suppressed in the USSR in 1927, still existed in exile. Since the Constantinople Conference in 1911, SCMs had been started in Greece, Bulgaria, Serbia and Romania; all had survived the war and were encouraged by a series of South-Eastern European Leaders' Conferences. Several foundered, as in Yugoslavia, only to be revived by the YMCA. The Federation persevered, however, in organising occasional gatherings of Protestants, Orthodox and Roman Catholics, and it was through such initiatives that the ancient Eastern churches, separated for so long, were drawn into the general ecumenical movement at its early stages.

Typically, Robert was not often present in person at the regular consultations in Britain between Orthodox theologians and others, yet Professor Leo Zander testified that no one was held in greater affection (for example, it was Robert who knew and cared about Zander's invalid daughter). His attitude was well expressed in the report of the WSCF European Council in Birmingham in 1937: 'the belief that ecumenism is not the triumph of any of us over any of the rest but the triumph of Christ over us all'[19] – indeed the phrase may well have been his.

On issues of academic theology in particular, Robert was happy to delegate to those he judged better qualified. During an interminable discussion on Barth at one Federation meeting, Fenn recalled Robert attending to urgent correspondence, but still regularly enquiring of him 'Is anything happening?' The answer continued to be 'no!'[20]

In a period when a re-emphasis on the doctrine of the church led many colleagues into various forms of 'high denominationalism', Robert's approach remained rooted in the reality of the local congregation. In an article in 1934 on 'Why go to church?' (it would be difficult to find a more unfashionable title) he writes:

> There is a solemn document known as 'The Interdenominational Position of the SCM' which contains this phrase: 'The SCM is in a particular sense part of the life of the Church.' That is not a decree from Lambeth; it is simply a truth which dawned upon us as we drew up the statement .... [Jesus] liked ordinary people, stupid people, bad people ... you will come to find the Cross more real just because it is all so ordinary, and men are so clumsy and halfhearted ... you are coming to God just as a man or woman who wants to begin again with others in a like case. There is something else you will find 'in a church' – that God is seeking to redeem the world through these queer assemblies of people with their all too familiar machinery of meeting one another over and over again ... once the courage, and the patience, and the love of one another which people have who believe in God, strikes home to you, you will never wonder about going to church again, you will be in the Church and you will seek to extend that fellowship which can never be content till all men are within it.[21]

On methods of outreach, evangelism and mission, Robert's annual reports to the General Committee reveal a questing and questioning spirit. In 1935 the official membership of the SCM reached an surprising 11,500 out of a total student population of

72,000; this did not, of course, include an extensive 'fringe' element which would not appear in its records. A D Lindsay, the Master of Balliol, judged that the SCM, through its 'national' activities, had produced a sense of student community which had not existed in Britain before. In *The Student Movement* of the same year, Robert wrote: 'Of set purpose we are not graded as Christians. It is dangerous to become an "evangelist" because it is so apt to put one beyond the reach of salvation!' And: 'The sudden outcrop of college missions – (tend[ing] not to reach outsiders but strengthen[ing] the faithful) – is a very interesting sign of the times ... what exactly it betokens I don't know. Is it a movement of the Spirit which will finally burst forth in a fresh turning of student life to God, or does it indicate a rather fevered condition in Student Movement branches, which know they are doing their job badly and want something to happen to relieve their consciences? I am in grave doubts about this.'[22]

Such comments were, of course, part of the normal shared assessment process which would follow any such event as the Edinburgh 'Religion and Life' Week when audiences averaging 700 listened to the Albert Schweitzer and Wilfred Grenfell, the latter subsequently to lead engineering students in building a necessary road in Labrador.

Like Tatlow before him, Robert remained firmly convinced that the appropriate methodology for a student movement was the study group, as a valid expression of its primary vocation. 'Right action springs from true thinking, and it is one of our principal concerns to reset study in the centre of our work as the primary organised means whereby our evangelistic task is carried out'; and again, 'Either we are going to have our movement based on the study group method or we are not'.[23] The alternative of the large gathering or action outside the academic community could be complementary, but could also be a distraction. Robert stood behind the efforts of the Study Department, and by 1937 the decision was taken to add to traditional study group leaders' training by the transformation of one of the two large summer Swanwick gatherings into a 'Study Conference', with the addition of library facilities and a longer more reflective programme. The introduction and development of 'Study Swanwick', which continued after the Second World War for a period, was one of the most creative innovations to come from the British SCM. Sadly, it has been too little imitated.

This emphasis was part of a growing concern for the university (or college) for its own sake, as a community with a unique function within the society in which it was set, a community charged with the transmission of learning and of specific values. Although other names came to be more closely associated with these concerns, such as Walter Moberly[24], Arnold Nash[25], Ronald Preston[26] and Marjorie Reeves[27], as early as 1931 Robert recognised intrinsic problems for Christians in this setting:

> ... an inability to see the vital relation of Christianity to academic work. Strangely enough this is a question seldom examined even by members of staff. A great many students simply do not know why they are at the university; there is absolutely no relation between the classes and life.[28]

In his 1934 report Robert makes his point with a quotation from Newman's *Idea of a University:*

> It is now possible to receive a university education without entering into any of the larger disciplines which would give it meaning. The vast majority of students are victims of specialisation on the same principle, if not to the same degree, as workers in a modern factory.[29]

In this, as in many other areas, he found the protestant approach overly individualistic – 'a preoccupation with problems of the individual's action'; 'Religion becomes a speciality for those who like that sort of thing'[30], a markedly accurate foreboding of the thorough-going privatisation of religion in the 1980s. From these beginnings there developed the Higher Education Foundation which still exists to promote similar concerns.[31]

Robert regarded himself as indebted always to the many 'ideas' people he worked with; but they, in their turn, appreciated his own sensitivity to 'grass roots' feelings and opinions. McCaughey quotes Fenn:

*When I joined the staff it was clear that many of the interests in which
the Movement was involved at the top were the interests of the senior
secretaries rather than of the Movement; and one of Robert Mackie's
gifts to us was his thrusting of such things back into the minds of
student committees to test them out as true interests.*[32]

Old Testament chroniclers recount how Solomon, on the eve of his
succession to his father David's throne, prayed for the gift of 'an
understanding heart', even more revealingly translated in the
Revised English Bible[33] as 'a heart with skill to listen'. This too was
Robert's frequent prayer, and there are numerous testimonies that
his request was heard.

Colleagues who welcomed the warmth and humour he brought
to the most routine meeting, might have been surprised, however, at the self-doubt and indeed depression which surfaced in
his commonplace books kept during the summer breaks with the
family at Biggar. When he wrote in 1936, ostensibly of student
members of the SCM, 'most leaders have an almost intolerable
sense of the difference between their aims and their achievements',
he spoke also for himself. 'There is in my heart a core of despon-
dency which inhibits me, preventing spontaneous joy of Christian
living' .... 'Is there not stronger, more imaginative leadership
than mine?' .... 'I am dumb this year. I do not think or speak
easily' .... 'An attempt to begin again. Not taking time, being
preoccupied, fear of my job, have again reduced me to barren-
ness. That was why I was dry for a Quiet Day, why I did not feel
I could help people personally. Lord forgive' .... 'Depression
because of sin and mistakes is our Gethsemane' .... 'How tired I
get of myself!' .... 'too shy, too reserved ... disabling ... fear in
relation to people .... All worry about myself is wrong it ought
to be replaced by repentance and a wider vision of God's purposes.'[34]

Kay Fenn has said that Robert possessed a faith in the goodness
of others which was surprising in one from a Calvinist tradition;
perhaps the legacy of that tradition is more evident in his own
personal spiritual struggles.

At the same time 'he made people happy – people were happy
with him.'[35] He remained constantly grateful for Dorothy's love
and support, but this was coupled with guilt that the demands

of his job, long hours and travel away from home, left her with unremitting responsibility for Steven. He seems to have been unaware that a sense of guilt for this circumstance was in itself, in that period at least, a sign of grace! 'Poetry,' he wrote, 'goes out of a busy life', but at Biggar again, 'Two wonderful sounds: a trickle of water at the bottom of a well, and bees in a lime tree'.[36]

In old age, Robert hugely underestimated his contribution as General Secretary to the British SCM. In conversation, in letters to him for his eightieth birthday, and to Steven after his death, ex-colleagues tried to find words to describe the difference he made.

Above all, he developed a genius for chairing committees, such an underestimated yet necessary practical and human skill in a more participative society. Typically, he saw it as an inheritance from his father. Eric Duncan sums it up:

> *Robert, more than anyone else I have ever known, emerged triumphantly from all the conferences, committees, minute drafting, project initiating, clarifying of others' muddled thoughts, at all of which he was such a master – emerged as a sensitive, profoundly understanding human being. Once in Geneva Visser 't Hooft said to me in some astonishment, 'Robert says he doesn't like administration! That is absurd! It's like Rembrandt saying he doesn't like painting!' I think Robert's secret was his utter and complete dedication of all his talents in a simplicity of spirit which was itself God's wonderful gift to him, and through him a blessing to us.*[37]

Notes to Chapter 6

1   They included F A (George) Cockin, later Bishop of Bristol; J W
     C Dougall, later General Secretary to the Church of Scotland's
     Foreign Mission Committee; A G Fraser, later Principal, Achimota
     College, Accra; Jean Fraser, later WCC staff, then Principal of
     St Colm's College, Edinburgh; A H Gray, popular Presbyterian
     preacher and theological writer; R O Hall, later Bishop of Hong
     Kong; Francis House, later WCC staff, then Archdeacon of
     Macclesfield; L S Hunter, later Bishop of Sheffield; K E Kirk,

later Bishop of Oxford; Frank Lenwood, later with the London Missionary Society in Benares and London; Florence Mackenzie and Helen Macnicol, both later Principals of St Colm's; Hugh Martin, Managing Director of the SCM Press; T R Milford, later Vicar of St Mary's, Oxford; Francis P Miller, later on the faculty of Yale Divinity School; J W Parkes, later ISS staff and inter-faith pioneer; William Paton, later Secretary to the International Missionary Council; R D Rees, later Secretary to the National Christian Council of China, then with the BCC; Ruth Rouse, later WSCF staff and historian of its early years; Agnes de Sélincourt, later Principal of Westfield College, London; W S Tindal, later professor at New College, Edinburgh; R D Whitehorn, later Principal of Westminster College, Cambridge; R P Wilder, later General Secretary to the Student Volunteer Movement for the USA and Canada; N Zernov, later Russian Orthodox Church visitor to British theological colleges.

2   SCM Archives: Selly Oak Colleges' Library, Birmingham

3   Letter from Robert to Tissington Tatlow, June 1933: ibid.

4   W D L Greer, General Secretary to the British SCM 1938-1945, later Principal, Westcott House, Cambridge, and Bishop of Manchester.

5   Report by Robert to Greer, 1937: SCM Archives.

6   Letter to Tissington Tatlow in *The Student Movement*.

7   SCM Press.

8   John R Mott.

9   WSCF Archives, Ecumenical Centre Library, Geneva.

10   SCM Archives.

11   'Christian Obedience in the University', page 46.

12   A prominent leader in the German church struggle, post-war Bishop of Hanover and a President of the WCC.

13   Mackie Papers.

14   'Christian Obedience in the University', page 28.

15   Scottish Secretary of the SCM, later a founding Bishop of the Church of South India, Secretary to the International Missionary Council (IMC), Associate General Secretary to the WCC and Director of its Commission on World Mission and Evangelism.

16   Letter from Eric Duncan and interview, 1991.

17   Outstanding French lay ecumenical pioneer, WSCF staff, founding

Associate Director of the Bossey Ecumenical Institute, key figure in the promotion of lay Biblical study.

18   Kay Fenn interview, July 1991.

19   WSCF Archives, Geneva.

20   Eric Fenn interview, July 1991.

21   Mackie Papers, Edinburgh.

22   Robert's staff report, 1937: SCM Archives.

23   Ibid.

24   Author of *The Crisis in the University* (SCM Press), and later Chairman of the University Grants Committee.

25   Author of *The University and the Modern World* (SCM Press), and later commuting professor between Britain and North America.

26   First Professor of Christian Ethics at Manchester University.

27   Vice-Principal of St Anne's College, Oxford, historian and pioneer of methods of teaching school history.

28   'Keeping Faith', 1931 General Secretary's Report: SCM Archives.

29   'The Exercise of Faith', 1934 Report: ibid.

30   'Making Plans to Measure', 1936 Report: ibid.

31   'The purpose of the Foundation is to analyse and develop an understanding of the underlying values and objectives of higher education, their philosophical basis and methods whereby they might effectively be pursued': Higher Education Foundation.

32   *Christian Obedience in the University*, page 19.

33   1 Kings 3:9 – *The Revised English Bible*, a revision of *The New English Bible,* published in 1989 by the Oxford and Cambridge University Presses.

34   Commonplace books: Mackie Papers.

35   Kay Fenn interview, July 1991.

36   Commonplace books: Mackie Papers.

37   Letter from Eric Duncan, 1979: Mackie Papers.

CHAPTER 7

The World as Parish

TO those who were close to the situation, Robert's move to become General Secretary of the World's Student Christian Federation in 1938 seemed a very natural progression, but it was less so to the man himself. At that precise point in the development of the ecumenical movement, however, the position was one of very considerable significance.

The establishment of the World Council of Churches was delayed by the outbreak of war in 1939 which created a 'limbo' context for the preparatory body, 'the Provisional Committee of the World Council of Churches in Process of Formation'. This was the outcome of more than half a century of growing understanding and co-operation which had seen the emergence of a spectrum of organisations such as the International Missionary Council, the World Alliance of Friendship through the Churches, the 'Faith and Order' and the 'Life and Work' series of consultations, and so on. It was, indeed, in just such an atmosphere that Robert himself had been brought up: his father's denomination, the United Free Presbyterian, was the product of the union of the United Presbyterian and the United Free in 1899, and the Edinburgh 1910 Missionary Conference was a watershed in the whole 'world church' process.

The form of the final 'umbrella' Council and its relationship with previous ecumenical bodies was naturally a subject of much debate. There were differing agendas, priorities and perceived functions. The earlier days had called for visionary and prophetic leadership; now, when the churches as institutions were setting up a comprehensive conciliar mechanism, there was need of diplomacy, patience and tolerance.

Not surprisingly, the man and the hour do not always coincide, but there was considerable unanimity in the choice of Visser 't Hooft for the key post of General Secretary, despite his youth. That tough, committed, experienced Dutch churchman had been General Secretary of the WSCF since 1932 and had, amongst other things, been a constant support to those leaders of the German SCM, such as von Thadden and Lilje, who had been closely involved in the Confessing Church's opposition to Nazism.

Visser 't Hooft saw the Federation as having been the main source of ecumenical education and consequently of knowledgeable leadership. He was thoroughly convinced of the need for it to continue in this role, a role that the churches themselves were not presently qualified to fulfil. He is credibly reported to have refused, for this reason, to take the new job unless Robert were willing to succeed him at the WSCF. The relationship between the two men was, therefore, of considerable significance for this next stage of ecumenical development. Robert was full of admiration for the theological expertise, the pioneering spirit, the leadership of Visser 't Hooft ('Wim'), and Wim's actions at this point and in 1949, when he brought Robert on to the staff of the new WCC as Associate General Secretary and Director of Inter-Church Aid, indicate the genuine value he placed on the other's gifts.

Marie-Jeanne Coleman, who knew both well, writes:

They truly needed each other and both knew it and appreciated it . . . . The cooperation between the two men was a beautiful thing to behold from WSCF days onwards.[1]

Another factor which lent significance and urgency to the Federation appointment, was the imminence of war. Unlike the outbreak of the First World War, which seems from contemporary evidence to have been largely unexpected by a generation used to the successful resolution of a series of international crises, the second loomed with an increasing inevitability as the 1930s progressed. Even an average British schoolgirl saw no hopeful resolution to the succession of events such as Japan's invasion of Manchuria, Italy's of Abyssinia, Hitler's of the Rhineland, the Austrian Anschluss, the Munich Agreement: the dread of approaching conflict provided an unwelcome backdrop to all our lives. And it is indeed disturbing to hear, in the current 1990s debate re assessing the causes and course of that war, suggestions that only hindsight has brought thorough understanding of such developments as the persecution of the Jews, when a general knowledge of the facts was readily available through the BBC, the more responsible newspapers such as the *Manchester Guardian* and the presence of numerous refugees in Britain and America, most obviously in universities.

Such information formed the context in which pacifist issues were raised in SCM and other circles. This made the discussion more sensitive and sophisticated than in the 1914–1918 period – though no less painful. In particular, those in the leadership of the Federation, such as Wim and Robert, had a peculiarly close personal experience of European events as the result of their friendship with and commitment to their colleagues in Germany, Czechoslovakia, Yugoslavia, Poland, France and beyond. All were wrestling with similar issues for Christian obedience in widely different situations: the matters were ones of life or death, the life or death of others or their own. In a time of uneasy peace, even more in a time of war, the reality and the preservation of this fellowship seemed paramount.

In the light of this conviction, and Wim's persuasion, personal preference for staying in Britain closer to his Scottish roots in a time of national danger, could not outweigh his sense of a more urgent ecumenical compulsion. So it was that the family left for Geneva and the WSCF headquarters in the Autumn of 1938. With very human inconsistency, Dorothy wrote a sad comment similar to the one she had made when they moved from Edinburgh to London a decade before:

> *I want to cry at the thought at leaving friendly, familiar London for some place so strange and remote as Geneva … it is good to have one's roots deep and to suffer in plucking them up, and good, no doubt, to have to do so from time to time. Mould should not grow on us yet!*[2]

In the event, her good conversational French, the helpfulness of colleagues, and the discovery – after strenuous search – of an attractive, conveniently placed villa to rent, meant that she was happily settled before Robert had to leave her alone for his inevitable travels.

The Federation General Committee in August 1938 had registered the unhappy, though not unexpected, news of the suppression of the German SCM by the Hitler regime: the last straw seems to have been the sponsoring of conferences, 'Evangelische Wochen', open to all church people and addressed by leaders of the Confessing Church.[3] The Munich compromise followed within weeks, and in October Robert wrote to his mother in Biggar:

I could not have imagined a worse time to begin a job, especially in Geneva. The heart has gone out of the international life of the city, and with the heart the brains have obviously departed from the League etc. There is a feeling of disillusionment ... there is a feeling that Czechoslovakia, Yugoslavia, Roumania, Hungary, Bulgaria will now rapidly make peace with the fascist states, and come to heel. From the point of view of religious freedom ... this will put the clock back in all Eastern Europe ... there is a feeling ... by Dutch, Scandinavians etc that this [is] the end of the independence of small nations, and that the only thing to do is to draw away from England and France and make friends with Germany ... they feel that European civilisation has received its death blow, and that we are slipping back to the dark ages.

At the same time he refers to a confidential German report and a letter from war-ravaged China, full of concern for European Movements, which move him to write: 'I am constantly humiliated by the affection and trust of much better Christians than myself.'

On a personal level, as he settled into a French, American, Chinese, English, Swiss, Dutch and Russian office team, accommodated 'in an old house, rather like some old family home in the High Street in Edinburgh', he found some solace in the fact that in Geneva, unlike Golders Green, 'when you get worried and depressed by human affairs, you can always get into the most marvellous world of nature'. At a meeting in the old League of Nations building, he 'sat looking at the evening light on the whole Mont Blanc range and was rather less attentive than [he] should have been'.[4]

Robert was convinced that it was essential for him to visit the Czech SCM before he left for his projected tour of India, China, Japan and North America. Consequently, he arrived in Prague in late October, to the surprise and delight of the Czech SCM, to undertake a round of meetings with groups of students and staff. As always, he saw himself as a 'channel' between movements, and in this instance he expressed both the general sympathy which existed at the victimisation of Czechoslovakia, and also, as faithfully as possible, the range of attitudes to events held particularly by French and British students. Of the Czech response he wrote: 'So great was the generosity of feeling that more than once apologies were made for their constant reference to the sense of betrayal and disillusionment.'[5]

The dominant request was to be kept in the mainstream of Federation life, a request answered characteristically by Robert on several levels at once – by the provision of a year's financing of their staff secretary (the previous source being no longer available), by a visit from Visser 't Hooft, now Chairman of the WSCF, and another from Suzanne de Dietrich to make up for the Czechs' inability to participate in the recent consultation on Bible Study training.

The subsequent complementary 't Hooft report is equally interesting but exhibits a revealing difference in tone, being more explicitly political and less personal.

> *The pre-Munich Czechoslovakia was one of the few countries in Europe in which democracy was not merely an accepted form of government but a living ideal ... it had become almost a religious passion.*

This last was not unappreciated by the Czech SCM leaders themselves; Robert had found them admitting that their movement had perhaps 'become too much a follower of Masaryk rather than of the Gospel'. Given the Czechs' expressed and singular faith in the League of Nations, Wim attacked the part played in particular by Lord Runciman, British politician and churchman:

... it sounds then either as an incredible naivety or as a ghastly joke when Lord Runciman – the man who could have known better than anyone else in the West what would be the outcome of a policy of compromise – writes to the Federal Council of the Protestant Churches in Czechoslovakia, 'I think that the Czech nation still holds in its own hand the government of its own affairs, that a happy and free Czech nation can live in the centre of Europe faithful to its old traditions and its best ideals'.[6]

The judgements carry an especial poignancy in the light of subsequent events – including the 'velvet revolution' of 1990 and the schism of 1993.

Robert attended the International Missionary Council in December 1938 in Tambaram, Madras, as one of a fraternal delegation from the Federation; this was followed by its Asian Leaders' meeting in Travancore in January 1939. ('It is an odd fate which makes me attend so many conferences, when I really dislike them from a personal point of view,' he wrote.)

He decided to take the opportunity to include visits to SCMs in Asia and North America, turning the occasion into a round the world trip. Dorothy accompanied him, and Steven was left at school in London. Pandit Nehru joined the 'SS Strathnaver' at Port Said and a previous London contact enabled Robert to arrange for him to meet 'an odd collection of his fellow-passengers':

... his statesman-like review of European politics and his handling of questions on Indian problems brought India herself and not British conceptions of India into the forefront of my thinking.[8]

Commitments prevented him from accepting an invitation for a prospective visit to Mahatma Gandhi and, also much regretted, a return to Bihar. But he remained aware of a different India he had briefly known and loved – different from the educated and Christian India which now so warmly welcomed him. He found himself on arrival 'garlanded like an oxen ... to the surprise of other passengers'.[9]

He was rather less aware of India's climatic variety; his friends, the Hollands, from the distinguished missionary family, remember him arriving on their doorstep dressed in shorts and shirt when the snow lay on the hills around.

Robert found the students 'Nehru followers to a man' and was 'a little embarrassed by questions on Mr Gandhi' [10], but he remained 'continually conscious of his [Gandhi's] presence on the Indian scene ... the prophet is still the force in modern India' [11] – the other India of the villages. He saw the Viceroy's palace as an affront to the surrounding poverty.

Two other Scottish friends present at Tambaram were Archie Craig – gentle, tough and humorous, with whom he had much in common – and George Macleod, whom he admired, but whose authoritarian style of leadership was so different from his own. Although much in demand as speaker and visionary, George Macleod had a somewhat patrician disdain for the SCM and its democratic ways. This did not disturb Robert, whose modesty was about himself and not about the causes and organisations which claimed his loyalty.

(Dorothy wrote from this trip, of Robert's likeness to his father: 'the immediacy with which he can grasp spiritual issues and be *sure* – even, as often in Robert's case, with all the *appearance* of uncertainty. Besides my own father I have never known anyone *so sure*).

Robert could enjoy a good Scottish Biblical wrangle: on this occasion, he wrote mischievously: 'On Sunday George Macleod preached a good sermon, though it was based ... on a misreading of scripture! Nothing daunts the gallant George!' [12]

As he met Indian SCM groups in different places, Robert was able to present the concerns of the European movements:

I say less of my own, so to speak, and tell them more and more of other students ... I am getting tired of my own ideas. It will be a treat to come back to Europe and talk about India. [13]

But the students found him more than merely a channel of communication. Dorothy commented: 'It is amazing how these lads just fall on Robert like a long lost brother and don't want to let him out of their sight.' The experience confirmed and reaffirmed the importance of contact between British and Indian students which the SCM had for long done so much to promote: 'I have preached the doctrine so often that I had forgotten how startlingly true it is.'[14] A very special kind of patience is required to go on repeating what goes on needing to be heard.

Robert was struck by the quality of the women students in particular, women who brought fresh skills. On observing the 'admirable' chairing of one particular meeting, he makes a wry remark: 'the men felt she did not *say* enough – a revealing comment!'[15]

The opportunity for a change in perspective on European affairs elicits the observation: 'we must not underestimate ... a West which ... contains many Christian ideas in its culture'[16] – a forecast of the current debate on the singularities of the relationship between Christianity and a post-Christian secularism.

Of the IMC conference as a whole he writes:

> *I wonder if it can be said that international Christian gatherings disappoint people in middle life but please the elderly, who see the advance which has been made, and the young, who see a vision for the first time ....*

and perhaps there are many who would endorse this conclusion from their experience of similar occasions. More profoundly, he continues:

> *My own chief impression is of persecution. I never realised before in my soul how Christians are suffering in many parts of the world. I came to realise it in some measure, not so much through harrowing details – often imparted confidentially – as through the reality of sympathy within our fellowship. The presence of Chinese and Japanese in the same discussions sharpened the feeling of pain and yet steadied one's faith in the church. Here was a fellowship which would stand an intolerable strain because, as an African put it, we have been brought together by the love of God .... There was little elation at the close of the meeting but, I fancy, much silent determination based on a new-found humility.*[17]

We gain an extra perspective on this trip from Dorothy's presence and consequent letters which reveal how little respite

Robert allowed himself, filling a call at Singapore with a pun-
ishing round of meetings to explore the possibilities of starting
an SCM – and the soil did indeed prove fertile. Typically, at
another stop he writes: 'I have had no time since we reached here
... and I have no more ideas! But the students are so lost and so
keen, that I can refuse no opportunity of speaking to them.'[18]

The journey went on to include 'Free China' at Kunming,
'International China' at Hong Kong and Shanghai, and 'Occupied
China' at Peiping, mostly by way of bucketting boat or over-
flowing third class train with wooden seats and live crabs and hens.
Robert, acutely aware of the multiple demands on Federation
funds, was always anxious to be as economical as possible on his
travels, a self-discipline not invariably shared by all westerners,
even if churchmen.

The three-day journey over the mountains from French Indo-
China to Kunming near the Tibetan border, called by the French
'L'Orient Extrème', allowed the usual making of friends: a cattle
truck (fourth class) turned out to be virtually filled with refugee
medical and engineering students. It was on one of these journeys,
along with Luther Tucker, a most able Federation Secretary from
the USA, that Dorothy made one of those sharp remarks which
delighted friends and somewhat disconcerted new acquaintances:
'Oh Luther, do be quiet, or they'll think we're all Americans!'[19]

The population of Kunming had been doubled, largely because
it had become home to three displaced universities, two from
Peiping and one from Tientsin. Robert found himself, as well as
consulting with local church leaders, addressing an audience of a
thousand in the open air. 'In spite of disabilities which seem almost
overwhelming,' he wrote in his travel diary for *The Student World*,
'the Chinese Universities are helping to create a new China, and
it was good to find ready appreciation of the part played by students
in other countries through the Far Eastern Student Emergency
Fund, and International Student Service.'

It is not possible yet to know the part that may have been
played by the efforts of the significant minority of Christian
students within these displaced universities, with their 'Religion
and Youth Weeks', in the later outstanding resurgence of a truly
indigenous Christian movement in China.

Leading six hundred students in a Hong Kong celebration of the Federation's World Day of Prayer, Robert commented: 'It felt like a British Quadrennial to sit on a platform with R O Hall, the Bishop of Hong Kong.'[20]

Everywhere he went, and this phenomenon could only develop with the years, he found ex-colleagues, students who had shared British or Federation experiences, and, perhaps most significantly, others who found his position as General Secretary of the WSCF sufficient credential in itself to elicit intimate fears and hopes. Perhaps the strangest encounter on this journey was with the Japanese customs officer monitoring his entry into occupied China; he turned out to be a member of the YMCA, whose student sections were affiliated everywhere to the WSCF. Undoubtedly, however, Robert's progress was undergirded by his never being 'off duty', as it were, at a cost to personal exhaustion which only Dorothy could see.

He was deeply impressed during his travels in China, Korea and Japan, by the solidarity of Christians across barriers of war and nationality. In Shanghai he visited a refugee camp, run by the Salvation Army assisted by Roman Catholic nuns, which had welcomed European Jewish fugitives:

Is there anything more scandalously inhuman ... than this hounding of unfortunates from Europe into that isolated and precarious settlement ... I don't think anything gave me so deep a sense of shame for our so-called European civilisation than the sight of these men and women being patiently received in the office of the National Christian Council of China – that last burden could at least have been carried elsewhere.

Again, on the Day of Prayer in Shanghai:

... our service was in the German Church ... it was typical ... on this first occasion when there was no SCM in Germany ... Chinese students, many of them refugees, should lead our singing beside a Holy Table with the inscription 'Ein Feste Burg ist unser Gott'.

The words were the very same sung by the crowd of German church folk barred by police from the SCM service in Darmstadt.

As Robert left he was given greetings to take to the YWCA in Japan 'in the name of our Redeemer'.[21]

In occupied China Robert met with the alternative problems, different but no easier, of those who had stayed behind: 'a dangerous task spiritually to carry on and yet a worthy one.' [22] Of Yenching University in Peking, he wrote: 'this university is not only Christian in name but producing many men and women of Christian conviction and character ... a couple of hundred ... are to be found in fellowship groups.' [23] Alert to the danger he could bring to his contacts, he wrote in hieroglyphics which Robert later admitted *he* had trouble in deciphering. 'In all this national effort there was never any evidence of hatred of the Japanese people only of "the system", "the military machine", *etc.*' [24] The embattled missionaries of Moukden welcomed communication with the outside world and Robert was able to serve as a confidential emissary for several.

He himself was distressed to receive information of European developments and exclaimed to his mother: 'I can't understand Chamberlain and Halifax saying they never expected this. All Europe knew it was inevitable that Czechoslovakia would be Nazified in some form or other, even when we left in November.'

Throughout the different Chinese territories, however, his experience of widespread conviction and constancy provided ample testimony – perhaps insufficiently appreciated by many – of the qualities which were to ensure the survival of the Chinese church in persecutions to come.

In Korea, also occupied by Japan, where the YWCA had made the decision to work with the Japanese YWCA, he found himself in the position of 'interpreting silences' and guarding his speech for the sake of others who risked much – and willingly – for the sake of his presence. (Police monitoring of Christian groups still occurred fifty years later from a different source of authority.)

The transition to Japan reveals Robert as acutely sensitive to the moral dilemmas arising from the contrasting situation. There was surprise to find one-eighth of the staff of the Imperial University Christian, and also to being

... seen off at the station ... by a medical professor with rich memories

of years in Edinburgh, himself the brother of the Minister for War ....
On no occasion in these days did anyone subject us to official propaganda
or attempt to put the case for Japanese action in China .... [Japan is]
a country in which loyalty is the primary virtue .... I find myself in dis-
agreement with some other recent visitors to Japan who have felt that the
Christian Church was wholly captured by national propaganda. I
found many evidences of disquiet in the minds of leading Christians and
of students. The constant appeal – 'What can we do to help Chinese
students?' – may sound hypocritical, but it is not. Here are words ...
pushed into my hand .... 'We neglect our Christian duty. We know
what we ought to do, what measures must be taken by us, but we have
not passion to do things that we believe to be true'.[25]

Robert makes the interesting observation that he found a real
sense of solidarity between the Chinese and the Japanese Christian
students; this he distinguished from some of the sentiments to be
found amongst missionaries who had so thoroughly identified
with the one or the other country that they applied pressure to the
IMC more overtly to take sides.

The subsequent tour of North America – from Vancouver
through Seattle, California, Texas, Washington, New York and back
to Greenock from Montreal – was a constant round of meetings,
speeches and making new personal contacts with many nights on
trains. One of the objects of the US part of the visit was a co-
operative attempt to discover the best form of association with
the WSCF for a hugely diverse Christian student movement which
included denominational activity on a vast scale alongside the
historically significant contribution of the YMCA and the YWCA.
(This was to lead to the establishment of the federal United
Student Christian Council – USCC.) Of one thing Robert was
soon convinced – no generalisation about any area of the work
was likely to be true owing largely to the particularities of each
state in its geographical separation. He was struck by the 'manner-
liness' of American students, by a 'complete absence of cynicism',
but also by a pervasive naivety rooted in isolation and conspicuous
prosperity. Fresh from the privations of the Chinese interior, he was
'almost shocked about the money spent on students'.[26]

Feeling increasingly inadequate to answer the barrage of

questions on the rapidly changing fortunes of the various European movements, Robert made a wry private comment to his mother on the capacity of some to combine condemnation of the British government's unwillingness to intervene more effectively in European events with an equally strong conviction that their own government should not do so. In addition, he was particularly struck by the apparent isolation from outside influences of the 'black' colleges, even within their own country. At one or two of these, 'I had a strange feeling of being taken to a missionary institution which I had not experienced at all, for example, in India'.[27]

The perpetual concern for Steven's welfare surfaces in every letter as the six months' separation draws to a close; as does an increasing exhaustion, clearly well concealed from his hosts – and Robert eagerly welcomes a break for Dorothy provided by the hospitable Francis Miller in Virginia. Appreciative of the generous responsiveness of so many to the multifarious needs expressed through the WSCF, even a measure of 'idealisation' of the Federation, he was determined to make it 'worthy of the confidence that many American leaders place in it' in terms both of its use of resources and also in the preservation and development of contacts.[28]

After their return to Geneva there was scarcely time to draw breath and to clear his desk before Robert was absorbed by the run up to the World Conference of Christian Youth to be held in Amsterdam from July 24th under the title 'Christus Victor'. This had been in preparation since 1935 through the co-operation of all the main world Christian youth organisations. With war imminent, even the tolerant Dutch authorities were nervous. They attempted to ban the speech by Reinhold Niebuhr on the grounds of 'communist sympathies', but they reckoned without their formidable compatriot, Visser 't Hooft:

> This strange accusation showed that the Dutch security organisation was not particularly competent in theological questions, for ... Niebuhr had rejected the communist ideology in no uncertain terms.[29]

In the final Conference Message the 1500 delegates, from virtually every country, affirmed:

*We know that we have met at a time of acute international conflict, and
we are grateful to God that it has been possible for us to meet at all ....
In war, conflict or persecution we must strengthen one another and
preserve our Christian unity unbroken .... The nations and people of
the world are drifting apart, the churches are coming together .... A
great responsibility rests on us to seek in our own countries ... for
closer co-operation in work and for larger sharing in worship with our
fellow Christians. The world needs a united church – We must be
one, that the world may believe ....*[30]

A young British delegate wrote:

*Within a month many of the journeys we had made to Amsterdam
would be impossible and we knew it. It was going to be war ... and we
were the youth who would be most involved .... Two and a half years
later I found myself a prisoner of the Japanese. We were a very mixed
lot in our camp, and the Christians were a very mixed lot too. I was glad
that I had already learnt a good deal about being one in Christ. I found
I was again forced to face the really important questions, and grateful
for the experience of Amsterdam that helped me to recognize them.*[31]

About twenty young Germans made their way clandestinely
(mainly by bicycle) to join their peers, and Visser 't Hooft recalled
a girl's reply as to why they had taken the risk – 'We could not
allow the church in Germany to go unrepresented. We belong
with you all.'[32] Later in his *Memoirs,* Wim was to write: 'I do not
believe that any large ecumenical conference has been so completely timely and relevant or has had such direct influence on the
life of the delegates.' In a letter to Robert dated January 1941
Wim described an instance of this:

*A young girl from Lithuania, who was at Amsterdam, decided ... to
escape ... and tells how she had to cross the frontier-country during the
night with the constant possibility of being picked up by Soviet soldiers.
Then she adds: 'I had two books with me, the one was the Bible, and
the other the Amsterdam list of delegates.' Think of the implications of
that story. Right in the midst of her danger she was accompanied by the
Word of God and by the crowd of witnesses.*

One of the new features of Amsterdam was an experiment in ecumenical worship which was to set the pattern for many post-war World Council Assemblies. Hitherto, the ban within Orthodox, Roman and Anglican church disciplines on an open invitation to share in the sacrament of communion had led to the exclusion of any such service at most ecumenical gatherings. Leo Zander of the Russian Orthodox argued that this practice, whilst apparently minimising denominational division, in actuality deprived everyone of a genuine understanding of the significance of sacramental worship in all the traditions. It was decided, therefore, to introduce full Reformed, Lutheran, Anglican and Orthodox eucharistic services; all were invited to attend but not to communicate, except for the essential 'open invitation' from the Reformed, which the others did not find themselves 'free' to accept. The great majority attended all the services and, for most, the Orthodox liturgy was a profound new experience. One delegate wrote, 'the atmosphere of mystic, timeless devotion and adoration gave an insight, otherwise unattainable, into the very soul of the Orthodox Church'.

The most difficult task of leading a united service of preparation for this painful experience of division was given to Robert, and there is no single occasion more often recalled both in recollections of Amsterdam and in later tributes to his influence. Everyone remembered his twin themes of repentance and hope:

Why can we not all be united at the common table in this conference? In this place we ought all to be one because we ought to be one Christian family. But we have failed .... Remember. It is the Lord's Supper. Jesus Christ is the host. Think not of your own irritation but of the agony in the heart of God. It is not <u>our</u> communion that is broken – it is the Body of our Lord Jesus Christ that is broken. And for that we must ask forgiveness. And yet – and this is the real miracle – He comes to our divided communion as Host. He takes our divided bread, and blesses, and breaks and gives. Whoever of us will be absent from any one of our communion services, Jesus Christ will be there.

There is irony in the fact that the official record lists his contribution to the event merely as 'Registration of Delegates' and 'Assistance with Conference Report'.[33]

Most of the student delegates then foregathered at Nunspeet to reflect and to share fears for the diversity of futures which were almost upon them. Robert told his mother how an African from French Togoland reported that his time in England and Amsterdam had changed his anti-European and anti-Roman Catholic position; indeed, the Africans as a group brought a note of 'conciliation amidst European bitterness'.

Robert speaks of the 'agony of spirit' of the Japanese who, touchingly, clung to him as one who had at least some understanding of the compulsive power of loyalty in their tradition:

> They said they could not condemn their country, for they were part of it, and shared the wrong it had done .... We are so apt to dissociate ourselves personally from any wrong our country does .... Britain and America came in for a good deal of criticism – as ever! .... Our self-righteousness – always pretending that we do everything from quite irreproachable and unselfish motives – is one of our great disadvantages ....

Robert concludes:

> The biggest impression is of religious seriousness. This is a generation which understands the Cross as my generation never did .... It has been a great experience even for a hardened soul like me![34]

On September 3rd war was declared in Europe.

Notes to Chapter 7

1   Letter from Marie-Jeanne Coleman to Nansie Blackie, 16.8.1993.
2   Letter from Dorothy to Robert, 28.1.1938: Mackie Papers, Edinburgh.
3   WSCF Archives, Ecumenical Centre Library, Geneva.
4   Letter from Robert to his mother, October 1938: Mackie Papers.
5   Notes by Robert on a visit to Czechoslovakia, October 1938: WSCF Archives.
6   Report by Visser 't Hooft on a visit to Czechoslovakia, 1938: ibid.

7   Letter from Robert to his mother, December 1938: Mackie Papers.
8   Notes by Robert on a visit to India, December 1938/January 1939: WSCF Archives.
9   Letter from Robert to his mother, December 1938: Mackie Papers.
10   Notes by Robert on a visit to India, 1938/1939: WSCF Archives.
11   Letter from Robert to his mother, January 1939: Mackie Papers.
12   Ibid.
13   Ibid.
14   Notes by Robert on a visit to India, 1938/1939: WSCF Archives.
15   Ibid.
16   Ibid.
17   Ibid.
18   Letter from Robert to his mother, February 1939: Mackie Papers.
19   Interview with Marie-Jeanne Coleman, July 1991.
20   Letter from Robert to his mother, February 1939: Mackie Papers.
21   Notes by Robert on a visit to China, February 1939: WSCF Archives.
22   Ibid.
23   Ibid.
24   Ibid.
25   Notes by Robert on a visit to Japan, March 1939: WSCF Archives.
26   Notes by Robert on a visit to North America, April 1939: ibid.
27   Ibid.
28   Ibid.
29   Memoirs of Visser 't Hooft: Westminster/John Knox Press, Kentucky, USA.
30   'Report of the World Conference of Christian Youth, Amsterdam 1939': WSCF Archives.
31   Post-Amsterdam reports: ibid.
32   Memoirs of Visser 't Hooft.
33   Post-Amsterdam reports: WSCF Archives.
34   Letter from Robert to his mother, August 1939: Mackie Papers.

CHAPTER 8

The Interpreter

FOR the first months of what was sometimes called the 'phoney' war, it was possible to travel freely and Robert took advantage of what could be only a temporary respite. He re-acquainted himself with opinions within the British SCM and found striking differences from attitudes during the 1914-1918 war:

> *The thing that Christianity should have prevented has happened and now Christianity is hard to apply …. The peace education of the past twenty years has done its work well and has produced a generation – in Christian circles in universities at least – with a wholesome aversion to war …. The general moral attrition of the last decade in international affairs has made the moral case for this particular war unreal …. The onus of decision has now been placed on those who do not wish to participate in war, and even that decision is not so drastic as it sounds since conscientious objectors are regarded as a legitimate category in the national life …. From the start, I found fundamental questions being asked … about the morality of any war … about the motives of the government … about any good coming out of this war, about Poland … about India etc. Above all, there was an entire absence of war-like emotion. I do not wish to suggest that there was any movement to avoid participation … many were waiting for their commissions or their summons to service and there was no marked unwillingness to accept military duties nor, on the other hand, was there any enthusiasm. Someone said to me, 'They put on uniform as if it were medieval armour, without much conviction that it will be effective'.*

He comments on the government policy which gave all clergy and theological students automatic exemption from conscription:

Certainly the church must conserve leadership but it will be very difficult to keep in touch with the troops. Strangely, it was in talking to older Christian pacifists that I found a deeper understanding of the real dilemma in the minds of the younger students.

Recalling Bonhoeffer's rejection of Reinhold Niebuhr's arguments that he should not return to a Germany on the verge of war, it becomes clear that there existed a widely-shared theology of involvement in the affairs of society, whatever form that involvement might take. This commonly-accepted attitude of responsibility may have had some bearing on the high quality of church leadership which was to emerge in the immediate post-war period. Robert's British ex-colleagues reassured him about the necessity for him to stay in post:

The movement is very conscious of its participation in a wider fellow-ship and shows its loyalty in many ways, not least financially .... The British SCM leaders do not remember the Federation occasionally as a queer enthusiasm which war has made irrelevant, nor do they sentimentalise about it, but quietly and determinedly they are thinking out their own position as British Christians in the light of their Federation membership.[1]

In January and February 1940 Robert circled North American campuses; in one typical instance he gave thirty talks in ten days. The main object was to describe and interpret the dilemmas and the suffering facing the European Movements – circumstances that American students often found difficult to understand, living as they did in a climate of isolationism and, in Christian circles, pacifism; not that Robert was insensitive to the latter, as long as it was based on knowledge and a realistic assessment of the cost of the different alternatives.

Increasingly the publication *The Student World*, of which Robert was now Editor, became central to the maintenance of such communication: 'It is imperative that [it] should in some measure fulfil today the function which Federation student conferences fulfil in times of the absence of war.' In the light of this conviction, he made strenuous efforts to secure 'an adequate range of opinion', although delays, censors, and the daily destruction of war were continual frustrations. In his first editorial in 1940 he wrote:

> *Some Christians find in war a Christian crusade believing that their cause is defending the interests of Christ and His Church; others, seeing in war a judgement of God upon their own nation as well as upon others, nevertheless take sides because they believe that certain principles of civilised life are being defended; others feel themselves so bound to their nation that they must unhesitatingly identify themselves with its cause in war, and perform their Christian duty in defending its existence; others regard war as blasphemy, and know that they can only take part in it, if they renounce their Christianity. Many Christians find themselves veering from one opinion to another, and hesitate to commit them-selves. How much truth is there in any of these opinions?*

Moving evidence of these costly and varied responses can be found in the reports of Suzanne de Dietrich as she travelled around France in the crucial spring of 1940. She quotes from letters sent to her:

> *War is a terrific absence of God and to speak of holy war is blasphemous but there are also so-called 'peaces' from which God is absent, states of peace where other wars are fought more ignominious than the one fought with weapons.*

From another:

> *A crusade? Certainly not. A 'just' war? Not in the strong and absolute sense of the word .... Without a doubt we must suffer ... from certain mixed motives in our cause and certain ambiguities in our propaganda; but there remains the fact that our States are striving to remain States true to their function and constitutions .... I have solid nerves but I was overtaken by anguish to the bowels when thinking of our brethren in Holland and Belgium .... If there is one thing I cannot bear ... it is this attitude, so frequent among us, which consists less in seeking to act in accordance with the will of God than to have a pure conscience. One does not spend time wrangling with one's conscience, discussing the ambiguities of every attitude, of all human action, when the whole of*

civilisation is at stake. I don't mean the Church, Christianity. The word of God will make its way for itself even under Hitler's foot – but this poor rest, this chance of a more human and just order ....²

A secondary but significant purpose of the American visit had been the raising of money for student refugees in Europe and China. Federation officers had foreseen that, somewhat in the pattern of 1914–1918, it would be of the first importance if war broke out in Europe to set up effective means of raising and distributing resources for both refugees and prisoners of war. Movements from neutral countries were clearly in the key position for this purpose. After his return to Geneva, Robert was able to put in train projects in several countries to assist Finnish, Polish, Czech, Hungarian, German, Spanish and French refugee students. (A wholly unexpected, but welcome, consequence came in the form of an invitation to visit the Finnish Movement, which had for over a decade been disapproving of the Federation's inclusive theological stance.) It was, incidentally, during this American trip that Robert began to feel he was at last succeeding in penetrating most of the areas of the United States, remaining fascinated by the differences between the various states. He found a pleasurable way of widening his own understanding of the American scene by reading relevant modern novels during the long night-watches on innumerable trains – a mode of transport undertaken because clergy tickets were available at half-price.

As hostilities in Europe spread, with the invasion of Denmark, Norway, Belgium, Holland and France, it became clear that Geneva itself was becoming in some sense a beleaguered city; there was general mobilisation of the Swiss army. 'The international churchmen' found themselves at the hub of a communications network in Europe's own 'civil war'. 'It is a time,' Robert wrote, 'when people feel so strongly, misunderstand so readily, and fall apart so easily.' In a letter to Francis House, an English Federation staff member who had worked in South East Europe but who was now unable to return to the area, he comments:

I see they are going to call up men of 41. I should not be interested in being a chaplain but I should be prepared to be a soldier, if I were

*needed. You see I feel my Christian job for now is with the Federation,
but God may want me to give up my specifically Christian job for the
practical one of helping my country . . . . . I am rather simple about such
things.*

It was decided, however, that the purposes of the Federation
would best be served if the staff were co-ordinated from Geneva
by the Chairman, Visser 't Hooft, whilst Robert made his base
in Toronto. This would allow him greater freedom of movement,
easier publishing facilities and ready access to New York.

On 16 June 1940, therefore, Robert left Geneva with Dorothy
and Steven, leaving behind his blossoming garden where he had
pruned and planted so happily, but perhaps also leaving, he hoped,
his recent rheumatism, the fruit of the local climate. They set out
by train en route for Bordeaux and Britain – then disappeared!
After six weeks of silence they returned to Geneva and told
their story: the train had broken down, France had declared an
armistice, and, after joining the crowds on the roads, sleeping on
straw in a schoolroom, they had been trapped in a small village
near Vichy as the German army took over. As Britain, unlike
France, was still at war with Germany, capture would have meant
internment, and they remained permanently grateful that no one
gave them away. However, Steven's twelve year old inclination to
practice his French and sketch army uniforms had been a little
nerve-wracking when they were eating at the same inn as German
officers. Cautiously, they managed to make their way back to
Switzerland by way of Lyon and Grenoble.

Delay seemed inadvisable, so they soon set out again, this time
with other refugees on a bus organised by an enterprising Swiss
travel agency, through unoccupied France to the Spanish border
and thence to Lisbon. At several points on this slow and tortuous
journey he was greeted by known and unknown Federation members who recognised him or his badge. In a village street, for
example, at the French/Spanish border, he was stopped by a
Russian, a keen member of his SCM, who was waiting for a train-
load of food from the USA for the use of refugees. In Lisbon he
succeeded in finding room on a small Portuguese ship, its only
drawback being that it had never crossed the Atlantic before.

I have felt my responsibilities for my family, and my work, and my country all the time, and often they have seemed to conflict .... I was amused and heartened by a comment of C S Tsai [a Chinese SCM colleague he had brought to work in England] .... 'It is good luck the big chief should suffer too – he would wish it that way'. Well we have just been on the fringe of suffering.[3]

On arrival in New York he was immediately drawn into some months of student conferences, councils, and committees organising refugee relief.

My casual British mind is always fascinated by the elaborations of American procedure, but student councils have the same characteristic the world over, a naive faith that the Kingdom cometh by discussion! I was not in good shape as a council visitor; my experiences of the summer, and the events in my own country, described with such painful vividness in the daily press, turned me into a sinister figure, which moved about muttering, 'Woe to the bloody conference!' But if I failed in detachment, others did not fail in sympathy.[4]

Suzanne de Dietrich, able to remain in touch with her beloved France, understood, and wrote: 'You must have to lead a kind of double life with one part of your heart and body in all kinds of discussions and committees and the other part in Britain and Europe – it is a hard strain.'

Then there was the setting up of a Toronto office as well as a family flat and a school for Steven. As Federation General Secretary, Robert was acutely sensitive to his obligation to be even-handed in his presentation of European issues in North America, whilst at the same time to be honest to the facts as he saw them. He felt that the premises on which the dominant American attitude of isolationism was based sprang from a misunderstanding of the course of international events, but was appreciative of the real willingness of Americans to listen to alternative interpretations. An insight into the kind of relationship he was able to create at astonishing speed emerges from a description of one occasion:

I recall one intelligent Christian pacifist who talked with me at intervals throughout a whole day and gradually came to realise that it might be possible for a fellow student to be in the army of his country in Europe and still remain a Christian. I felt that I was privileged to be in touch with a spirit which was out on a great and dangerous adventure that day.[5]

From his 'Travel Diary' in *The Student World:*

The world outside is a great disappointment to young America. I often found myself marvelling at generosity of spirit, and unable to understand its origins. I suppose the lesson always to be learnt is that God speaks to every people in his way, and not in your way.

Robert saw a most significant mutuality in the involvement of the North American movements with the WSCF:

Through the window of the Federation American students are prepared to look at the work of the church in the world. American students are prepared to look at <u>theology</u> through the window of the Federation. Certain Christian experiences which seem remote to them are worth studying because they are real to their fellow members in some other country. All this places an immense responsibility on the leaders of the Federation in America and throughout the world.[6]

Robert's reception in Canada was naturally much easier as Canada itself was a belligerent in the war alongside Britain, though the problem of distance still remained. It was, however, and continued to be, a real burden to be safe and comfortable when reports of the London 'blitz' made the headlines.

In Toronto he felt the lack of colleagues and sufficient support in the office, in spite of considerable assistance from Dorothy; to Francis House he comments wryly: 'I have really been rather badly brought up because I have always had an office run by other people!'; and to Wim and Suzanne: 'I think you over-estimate my ability to carry on as an adequate representative of the Federation. I miss the Geneva background and the meetings more than I can say. It is astonishingly difficult to be a secretary of an international movement all by oneself, so to speak.' Suzanne writes to Francis:

'he carries a heavy and solitary load and the strain of being cut off from Britain and Europe is hard on him.'

It became difficult to reconcile the competing demands of Editor, administrator, preacher, promoter, mediating committee man and regular commuter to New York.

Unless you 'promote' a movement on this continent it gets forgotten. The size of America has much to do with it. It is hard when people say – probably with reason – that a few visits would produce 10,000 dollars more for the relief of refugees and prisoners, but I am in terror of over-tasking myself spiritually as at the moment I have done physically.[7]

He was relieved when his efforts were complemented in October 1940 by a six months tour of India and China by Helen Morton, an American Vice-President of the Federation.

For Dorothy this was not a very happy time for quite natural reasons: Britain was largely isolated and threatened with invasion. She was often alone with her dread and concern for family and friends in Scotland. At the same time she had to help Steven to come to terms with a very good but large and strange school, and both had some episodes of ill-health. She was appreciative of extensive Canadian kindness but found few intimates to share her intellectual interests. Marooned in a casually comfortable society, she adopted, partly from necessity but also from principle, quite a spartan life-style with second-hand clothes and Woolworth Christmas presents for Steven. Her letters to Robert's sister, Janette, reveal her concern at British domestic difficulties over such things as food rationing; they also include a little mutual self-mockery: 'It amused me that you find it hard not to have a light dress convenient to change into at night. I suppose we all have our traces of gentility that cling to us even in a war!'

Sent by 'decisions of committees' (and following John R Mott, who had toured in 1940), Robert spent May and June 1941 in Brazil, Uruguay, the Argentine, Chile and Peru:

Five New Nations. They were new to me, and I found them new to themselves. They pointed out that their real history was ahead of them; and I, with my mind full of history ending in Europe, was quickly caught up in their enthusiasms .... I might have been setting out for the lost continent of Atlantis for all the knowledge I possessed, as I stepped on board ship with my bag full of books ... about Latin America. But all my rapidly acquired knowledge was thrown out of gear by taking to the aeroplane. Flight removes all sense of proportion; it is very upsetting to arrive too quickly at your destination.[8]

It was good for my soul to cease for a time to be a 'pundit' because I was a visitor from the outside, and became rather, an interested spectator, whom the wind had blown in!

Visa restrictions and limitations of time and organisation under-mined the value of his journey in his eyes, but at the same time gave birth to the desire to encourage the emerging student groups:

In a disintegrated university they must draw students together and give them a sense of solidarity. This they must achieve in the name of Christ, whose followers in the organised churches are often relentlessly hostile to one another. Their danger will always be to become either an evangelical coterie, or a vaguely religious club. A miracle of fellowship is required and I saw signs of its beginning.[9]

Robert was struck by 'the quick expression of a common concern' by two or three Roman Catholic leaders with whom he had con-versations. 'It is precious little that we (the WSCF) have done, and time alone will show what we can do. But in all three at least of the countries I visited I found men who profoundly believed in it.'[10] He would have been unaware of the phrase used of him by a new friend made during the trip – 'the sympathy he radiates.'

From this time Robert harboured the hope, unfulfilled, that one day he might be given the chance to immerse himself more thor-oughly in the region. He was fascinated in Peru by the evidences of 'that timeless history which has no beginning or end. I saw burial robes of surpassing beauty, woven in pre-Christian days, and I was sick at heart that I could see, and understand, so little.'[11]

Meantime, in the German occupied Netherlands the SCM dissolved itself rather than conform to the law forbidding organ-isations to include non-Aryan members, and several church

leaders took care not to sleep in their own beds. Visser 't Hooft
wrote:

> ... we have the curious situation that continental Christianity discovers
> that faith demands concrete decisions at the same time as the people
> of the Social Gospel [the Americans] suddenly become other-worldly,
> though the other world in which they live is not the transcendent
> world.[12]

A survey of national SCMs written in 1944 comments:

> It was not the Dutch university that made a stand against the ideological
> claims, Leyden excepted ... it was the students, only in a few cases
> preceded by their teachers ... the real resistance came out of the student
> ranks. The Dutch university, sharing the destiny of the modern university
> in general, possessed no clear confession, it had withdrawn itself in a
> vague perilous neutrality. A few instances excepted, it did not know
> what it stood for ... incoherent, without a distinct notion of common
> convictions ... common traditions.[13]

In France, Suzanne reported being 'moved deeply' by the action
of German friends who facilitated the appointment of French
pastors to French prisoners of war – 'it makes our ecumenical
fellowship very real.' The moral dilemmas were different in the
occupied and the unoccupied areas: 'distinctions must be made,'
wrote Wim, 'between the kind of collaboration with Vichy which
takes place in the realm of youth work and the kind of collaboration
which takes place in the political realm, for there is a world of
difference between the two.'[14] In February 1942 the French SCM
succeeded in holding a conference for 200 students in unoccupied
Grenoble and ran a university mission.

Of Britain, however, Visser 't Hooft wrote somewhat ambiva-
lently in October 1942 that it was 'far too happy and comfortable
a country to have the true perspective on the situation but ... [it]
has still a remarkable detachment and a capacity for dispassionate
thought which has become very rare in the modern world'.[15]
William Paton, however, felt that the isolation of Geneva had left
him with little understanding of British developments.

In many of the countries most under pressure the SCM and the churches found a new solidarity in suffering. Einstein had written:

> *When the revolution came to Germany, I looked to the universities to defend freedom, knowing that they had always boasted of their devotion to the cause of truth; but no, the universities were immediately silenced. Then I looked to the great editors of the newspapers and to the individual writers of Germany who had written much and often concerning the place of freedom in modern life; but they too were mute. Only the churches stood squarely across the path of Hitler's campaign for suppressing truth. I had never had any special interest in the Church before but now I feel a great affection and admiration because the Church alone has had the courage and persistence to stand for intellectual truth and moral freedom.*

Of major concern in the Canadian context were the needs both of prisoners of war and residents in internment camps. Robert initiated contacts with the camp authorities and the Red Cross, raising funds in the US and Canada itself, and then found Dale Brown, an American conscientious objector with similar experience in Cuba, to work full-time for the International Student Service (ISS) out of the Federation Toronto office, providing books and services including relevant university courses where possible. Similar efforts were pursued throughout Europe and China.

The difficulties involved in such work lay not only with combatant governments and the conditions of war, but also with the harmonisation of organisations and methods in Europe, North America and Asia. By 1943 World Student Relief, based in New York, provided resources for European Student Relief (the co-operative association of the ISS, the WSCF and Pax Romana, the Roman Catholic international student secretariat), similar projects in the Far East and the camps. Experience since the 1920s with the International Student Service, itself an extension of earlier WSCF relief involvement, and a personal knowledge both of the officers of the different organisations and of the countries concerned, gave Robert a unique insight into the possibilities and problems. It was a hard but necessary apprenticeship to his post-war role with the WCC.

It is impossible, however, not to resent somewhat on his behalf, the endless memoranda, meetings, travel and diplomacy needed to achieve the required co-operation. That said, the contacts involved through World Student Relief extended even more widely the influence of the WSCF itself, as, for example, when Roland Elliot went from New York to Yenan as an envoy for WSR. His meeting there with Mao Tse-tung and Chou Enlai engendered a new and mutual trust which facilitated the later development of the China Christian Council under the leadership of K H Ting.[16]

In spite of all the difficulties and delays in communication Robert in Toronto found himself throughout the war the centre of a world network which spanned battle fronts and neutral frontiers alike. This it is which informs and enriches his contributions to succeeding issues of *The Student World*, reflecting the changing events and his perceptions of them. Each quarterly issue addressed a specific theme. At the end of 1942 it was 'Christian Responsibility in Wartime'. On this he begins:

> *Upon this student generation have fallen strange and terrible responsibilities in action and in suffering. In heart and mind the times are testing them. Beyond the war, and yet beginning now, lies another responsibility, in which we must not fail, or all this agony will have been in vain. We ask our God for hearts and minds in which a human order more in accordance with his will may be built, and in which it cannot break down, because the mind is open to the light, and the heart to the strength, of his Spirit.*

Later he writes:

> *An obvious tendency of students is to analyse their problems until they are reduced to frustration. Partly it is the fault of their being plunged in peace time into a speculative and argumentative atmosphere before they have met much experience that is worth thinking about. Partly it is the result of having no adequate faith with which to face life squarely. Human problems are solved not on paper but in life ... now ... our problems must be faced and not merely discussed ... thousands of students have found themselves lifted out of a restricted academic world into the varied and unselected community of the armed forces, of*

*prisoners of war and refugee camps and of conscientious objector camps.
Here a much closer identification with the community is demanded of
the student and of universities. Certainly this is most clearly seen in
China, where the destruction or enemy occupation of university buildings has led to an enormous student migration. Students find themselves
not only improvising the means of continued study but living much
more realistically in the total community, struggling and suffering with
it ... communities which otherwise would have been totally unaffected
by the existence of universities .... Whereas there have always been poor
students, now a whole student community, as in Athens at this moment,
may be reduced to the level of starvation .... There is surely an unparalleled opportunity of facing frankly 'la trahison des clercs'. Unless
our universities can provide a basis in education and character for new
human relationships, and an unparalleled spirit of service to the community, they had better close their doors .... In the WSCF we have
made some discoveries in living together as nations and races. We know
where some of the prejudices, the blind spots, the sensitive areas lie
.... We have learnt to be concerned for one another and to think in terms
of the common good. This is one of the great political problems of the
future .... Are America and Britain for example prepared not only to
give all their own citizens a better chance but to give the unknown
citizens of other countries a better chance, even, if necessary, at the
expense of their own?* [17]

Looking back, Robert realised: 'by 1942 I was clearly very
unsettled. This was partly because I felt "out of the war effort"
and partly because I began to be offered jobs in Scotland and in the
International Missionary Council. Dorothy stood by and steadied
me in a wonderful way.' She wrote to him:

*I don't believe for one minute that anyone else can hold that particular
position – [the General Secretaryship of the WSCF] – and the fact
that it is a continual struggle and pain to you may be just the reflex
side of a definite contribution God asks of you to the work of the
Christian Church now and hereafter. Peace of mind can be purchased
too dearly ... we were led out into a far country for a reason.* [18]

The welfare of the members of the German SCM, such as

Hanns Lilje, remained a constant concern, and in April 1943 Dorothy wrote:

> ... *you must never forget that in doing your present job you are doing something for him* [Lilje] *and these invisible brothers which you could not really do in your own country .... I feel that if the news should reach him that you had left the WSCF he would feel that something had slipped in the outside world. I believe that to him and his kind the WSCF is now you and Suzanne and Wim. The two latter are not free people because of their country's position. You are, and you have chosen, and because he knows YOU and trusts you he knows you are perfectly true to him and his. This seems to me so big a thing in the world of eternal values that you must be content to face and overcome all your very natural restlessness, in which I do sympathise with you, you know how deeply.*

Dorothy's health remained a concern and in 1943 she underwent a hysterectomy from which convalescence was slow. On extended journeys, with all the delays and hazards of war-time, Robert was frequently dependent on her translating, editorial and administrative skills. On the train to Halifax to join a convoy to Britain in November 1942, he wrote that she was:

> ... *the ideal colleague ... for you share my judgement and have my absolute confidence. Few men can have a partnership like mine .... It is wonderful how we become increasingly drawn to one another, so that we have most of ourselves in common. All the best things about marriage and family cannot be said in books .... I shall try to be faithful to you and God in every way with some knowledge that when I fail I do not fall out of your love or his.*

At the same time he acknowledged that leaving her and Steven so often 'tears the heart out of me'.

As usual, Robert treated this first travel by convoy in the north Atlantic as a learning opportunity and emerged full of admiration for the seamen who regularly dodged submarines, 'shepherded by the destroyers and corvettes of four nations'. His cabin-mate turned out to have heard him speaking to students in Kyushu;

initially Robert had given Dorothy a rueful description of 'a young, zealous evangelical – mouth, eyes and hair! reading one of Andrew Murray's books, and underlining it ominously!', but … 'we got on splendidly by a system of mutual respect. I have learnt much from him. Theologically we are pretty far removed from one another, but not spiritually.'

He befriended the more vulnerable of his fellow passengers and disrupted his own arrival at a 'blacked-out' Liverpool by finding accommodation for them all. 'One thing will be good,' he remarked, 'to sleep out of one's clothes.' Next morning 'in the black-out I was seeing Mrs B the widow lady off to Watford – a great load off my mind – 13 pieces of luggage including all the deceased husband's clothes, and the bed of the dog left behind! A nice woman who may go quite batty. I had wired Billy [Greer] that I should travel on today, but I suddenly found that the Newfoundland nurse lassie was scared stiff … her boyfriend had to be wired too, so I promised to wait and see her fixed … pages from the life of the successor of John R Mott!' [19]

On this long coveted visit home, Robert was to discover that the breadth of his experience in the previous four years, reinforced by his peculiar capacity to respond to people and events, had widened his perspectives in such a way that he was frequently unhappy with the attitudes even of some of his closest friends. In a few of his previous SCM colleagues, he finds 'British dogmatism unshakable …. Their world contains no insoluble mental and moral problems'. They found him 'too much affected by experiences in Europe …. Now I feel just stupid, without a home or a policy or a leg to stand on'. Again, 'I found considerable misunderstanding of the States …. People are sensitive on US being critical about India – and yet there is truth in the criticisms …. My tendency to stand up for the losing cause put me in a queer place …. Being an interpreter is hard.'

On a personal level, Robert found he was used as a 'safety valve' by SCM staff who had preferred his enabling style of leadership to his successor's more authoritarian approach – 'He is a leader and knows where he is going. I never did, never do'; this troubled him as he was above all anxious to be of help to Billy Greer and he was acutely aware of his own defects and the other man's strengths.

'My hope is that I can hold the Marxian revolutionary crowd, and the Barthians here in loyalty to the WSCF without alienating the old guard.' He was confirmed, however, in the opinion that the decision to locate in Toronto had been the right one: 'I am clearer than ever I could never have carried on the WSCF from here.'

He gave what time he could to his mother, mother-in-law and sister-in-law. On Christmas Eve he wrote from Biggar, 'I feel very homesick here, since every corner speaks of you and Steven to me. This is our little town not mine particularly'. He retraced long walks in the hills: 'It was fine to be properly tired, as I had not been for three years – tired and yet invigorated. The colours are the special gift of our countryside. Some ploughed fields are blood-red and yet the prevailing colours were blues and browns.'[20]

In February 1943, shrouded in military and diplomatic secrecy, Robert even achieved a hazardous journey by air from Leuchars in Scotland to Sweden, 'all dressed up in life-belts and parachute equipment'. As Sweden was neutral, it was possible for him to meet emissaries from Wim who had left Geneva the same day, bringing uncensored and confidential news of the different European SCMs. Here he heard reports of their involvement in resistance movements: how, for example, the proscribed Dutch SCM had twice the outreach of the pre-war period. He reminds Dorothy of their affection for Geneva: in Stockholm: 'The river is like the Lake of Geneva, and the bridges and buildings make me think so much of our own home city.'

Once again, however, he finds himself driven by the demands of a global loyalty to uncomfortable disagreement with colleagues: on questions of student relief he argues by cable with Geneva: 'Wim thinks in European and Church terms; I have to think in *world* and *Christian* terms. The hardest thing is to be seen to cross them when I want to express all loving allegiance.'[21]

Back preaching in Biggar in March before his return to Canada, Robert commented: 'I said this morning that from Europe came a challenge of evil [in Nazism] and also a challenge of grace in the Church. I am thrilled all over again at the nature of the widespread and united Christian resistance. I leave with a new sense of mission.'[22]

In January 1944 further travels in Peru, Chile – where a new Movement had started – Uruguay, Brazil and Mexico, elicited continuing fascination with their histories and cultures and admiration for many individual Christian leaders, both Protestant and Roman Catholic; but also a deep concern for the regeneration of the churches of south America, their relationship with each other and with society as a whole. Robert made lasting friendships but felt he did not accomplish a great deal, referring ruefully to their patience 'with me as a globe-trotting, hotel-staying caricature of a Christian'.[23] From a later perspective, however, it is possible to see in these painstaking visits, following as they did those of Mott and Suzanne de Dietrich, the start of a slow process which brought marginalised and conservative Latin American Protestant groups into the mainstream of ecumenism and of social concern – so much so that, in the 1960s, they became a major seed-bed of 'Liberation Theology'.

The entry of the USA into the war after the events of Pearl Harbour naturally brought about a vast change in public mood. The over-reaction of the US Government in its treatment of Japanese-Americans, now much regretted, brought an immediate response from the American SCM in protest and in subsequent care for the interned on the West Coast, much to Robert's admiration. He continued to use the pages of *The Student World* as his chief method of interpreting the feelings and attitudes of European and American students to one another.

Americans early became concerned with problems of the future and reconstruction whilst the Europeans were understandably preoccupied with present danger and suffering. In time for the Universal Day of Prayer for Students, observed with a particular sense of solidarity during these years, he wrote 'A letter from the Editor to his friends in Europe', explaining that such different attitudes

> ... *are not in opposition, they are complementary. The most wonderful thing to my mind is that in our thought and conversation we are so conscious of one another ... it is not our experience of war and disaster which unites us, but our experience of Christ .... Christians have not only a peculiar obligation in times like these to think realistically about the*

future, they also have a flying start. We can talk with one another, while the secular world has no language it can use .... *Perhaps the very fact that we do not try to make up our minds alone as national groups is the first step towards a Christian view of the world* .... *My task on this continent has been to try to interpret suffering, such as I have not experienced, to others who can scarcely imagine it* ... *the effort on the part of student leaders to raise money for the relief of suffering amongst students in China and in Europe is based on a genuine desire to associate themselves with suffering* .... *And in the years ahead you will need him – the American – as badly as he will need you.*[24]

Robert expressed himself as so at home by now in the North American context that he felt he might venture into print with an analysis of the difference in perspective of the American and the British SCMs:

The alternative to theology in the American SCM is democracy. Instead of wrestling with ultimate verities, you make lists of the ideas which have drifted into your mind. Instead of waiting with solemnity upon the will of God, you go through the complicated process of deciding by ballot. In a curious way theology is expected to grow out of democracy which is in itself the precious and ultimate truth. That may be a caricature ....

He was not the first or last Briton to question the American faith in democratic mechanisms, nor the first to find it accompanied by a greater openness to such criticisms than would be common in Europe. Recalling Robert's own reservations about theology (he spoke of 'that peculiar form of cynicism which takes refuge in endless theological analysis'), it is not altogether clear where his own sympathies lay; probably, as usual, they were divided. This seems all the more likely when he adds: 'If the eighth chapter of Romans is the key passage for the British SCM, the American student finds his starting point in the story of the Good Samaritan.'[25]

In October 1944 it became possible for Robert to cross the Atlantic again, and for Wim to come to London to meet him and plan for the future. He wrote to Dorothy that Wim 'went out of his way to say that *The Student World* has been magnificent. That gave me more pleasure than any other remark'. After much frustrating delay over visas, Robert was able to achieve meetings in Paris and Geneva, be reunited with colleagues and meet a new one of whom he wrote to Dorothy: 'Marie-Jeanne de Haller[26] is quite charming. I loved her instantly, so natural and so gracious. She will be a real friend .... Obviously Europe needs me a little, because it needs more than theology ....'

As the war drew painfully to its end, first in Europe and then in the Far East, themes of reconciliation and reconstruction gained prominence both in *The Student World* and in the lives of the different Movements. By the end of 1945, after a tour of Sweden, Norway, Finland and Denmark, Robert was back at his desk in Geneva and the temporary headquarters of the WSCF in Toronto had been closed.

Notes to Chapter 8

1   Notes by Robert on a visit to Britain, October/November 1939: WSCF Archives, Ecumenical Centre Library, Geneva.
2   Suzanne de Dietrich's report from France, 1940: ibid.
3   Letters from Robert to his mother, August 1940: Mackie Papers, Edinburgh.
4   Letters from Robert to his mother, September 1940: ibid.
5   Notes by Robert on a visit to the United States, 1940: WSCF Archives.
6   Letter from Robert to Dorothy, October 1940: Mackie Papers.
7   The Editor's 'Travel Diary', *The Student World*, 3rd Quarter 1941.
8   'Impressions of Student Life in South America', *The Student World*, 4th Quarter 1941.
9   Ibid.
10 Ibid.
11 Letter from Robert to Dorothy, June 1941: Mackie Papers.
12 WSCF Archives.
13 Ibid.
14 Ibid.
15 Ibid.

16 K H Ting, outstanding Chinese Christian leader, WSCF staff
    1948-1951, Anglican Bishop and President of the China Christian
    Council.

17 'The Challenge to Political Responsibility', *The Student World*, 4th
    Quarter 1942.

18 Letter from Dorothy to Robert, 11/11/1941: Mackie Papers.

19 Letters from Robert to Dorothy, November 1942: ibid.

20 Letters from Robert to Dorothy, December 1942/January 1943:
    ibid.

21 Letters from Robert to Dorothy, February 1943: ibid.

22 Letters from Robert to Dorothy, March 1943: ibid.

23 Letters from Robert to Dorothy, January 1944: ibid.

24 *The Student World*, 1st Quarter 1943.

25 The Editor's 'Travel Diary', *The Student World*, 4th Quarter 1943.

26 Marie-Jeanne de Haller, notable member of WSCF staff, later to
    marry a Canadian colleague, John Coleman, appointed in 1945 to
    promote the Federation's concern for the nature of the University.
    Later he became Professor of Mathematics at Queen's University,
    Kingston, Canada.

CHAPTER 9

The Road back from War

THE theme of Robert's first editorial for *The Student World* in 1946 is indeed appropriate for the whole of his concluding period as WSCF General Secretary. Under the heading 'The Road back from War', he wrote:

> *Out of the armies and the resistance, out of prison camps and hiding-places students are marching on the road back from war .... There is no single judgement that can be made on this vast human upheaval, save that the agony of war shows with stark clarity the good and evil that is within man, and reveals unmistakably the strength and weakness of the Christian Church .... Faith matters more; for some men now know they lack it, and others have found it for the first time. Unbelief and belief are nearer to one other than either is to indifference .... The Church has failed and it has succeeded. All public manifestations of Christianity seem a hollow mockery against the background of total and relentless warfare. Protestations of Christian love seem blasphemous when men, women and children die in cattletrucks or pens not fit for beasts. It is a sound instinct which makes men recoil from the self-righteousness of an institution which was created for the world's salvation and only succeeds in saving itself. And yet the Church has had its victories. Not once nor twice it has led a resistance or redeemed a sordid moment. Through the faithfulness of its members it has brought light and comfort to the souls of men in torment.*

He concludes:

> *The courage and conviction of abnormal days are apt to seem like ancient suits of armour in the so-called normal world .... There will be*

*no smooth passage for the movements which welcome the war generation,
but there will certainly be a wind in their sails. For these men and
women have discovered that the world is worse than ever they expected,
and the only Christ who interests them is one who can save to the
uttermost. They can teach us great lessons on their road back from war.*

In August 1946 it was possible to hold the first Federation
General Committee since 1938; this took place at the newly-
founded Ecumenical Institute at Bossey, outside Geneva. Nothing
was easy about the re-establishment of relationships between recent
combatants, a process made more difficult by the totally different
experience undergone by the occupied, the unoccupied, the
imprisoned and the neutral, the victor and the vanquished. The
final statement on 'The Relationship between Victorious and
Defeated Nations', long and strong in language, was no formal
theological affirmation, but a declaration of faith forged in the
fire of personal suffering and painful hours of controversy.

> *The national-socialist and fascist dictatorships with their system of violence,
> violation of pledges, atrocities, bestial cruelties, racial arrogance and
> claims to the hegemony of one people over its neighbours have brought
> immeasurable suffering to the nations .... On the other hand it must
> not be forgotten that other nations also shared in the responsibility for
> the growth and terrible consequences of the totalitarian systems. Through
> their own selfishness, passivity, opportunism and lack of unity and
> vision .... Convinced that in this sense we are all guilty before God and
> continually victims of the same temptation, the Federation lays on the
> heart and conscience of all its associated movements and their members
> the necessity of examining before God their past and present conduct,
> and confessing their sin against God and men .... It is only through
> the forgiveness of God, which calls us at the same time to mutual
> forgiveness, that the wonderful gift of a completely new beginning
> and true fellowship is bestowed. This fellowship has not only a personal
> significance ... but ... is a new creation of incalculable political
> importance in an age when mankind is preparing to take the path of
> moral and physical self-destruction.*[1]

The meeting demanded all Robert's particular talents for

mediation and reconciliation. A most welcome arrival at the General Committee was vice-chairman Reinold von Thadden, released from ten months imprisonment in a Russian Arctic camp for political criminals. His lay status had made him particularly vulnerable after he became one of the ten signatories of the document sent by the Confessing Church to Hitler in June 1936, challenging Nazi ideology and practice in the name of the Gospel; indeed he was arrested by the Gestapo in 1937.

Field Commander of Louvain during its German occupation, von Thadden had the unique distinction of being honoured by its citizens after the war for the protection he had afforded them. He was markedly qualified to write on 'God is Faithful':

As Mont Blanc shrouds its snow-capped peak in the clouds for weeks at a time and remains invisible, so that we quite forget its existence in the landscape, until the moment when the giant unexpectedly casts off its veil, and stands there before us in all its power and indescribable majesty, so God likewise remains the DEUS ABSCONDITUS (Luther), inaccessible of approach to all our intellectual efforts and passionate longings. And then, one day, when the need is greatest, he comes forth from his hiding place, the DEUS REVELATUS (Luther), and makes it overwhelmingly clear that he is there and has already long since taken all our cares, all our heartache, into his almighty and merciful hands.[2]

The same autumn Robert made his first post-war visit to Germany, recalling as he did so his visit as a student under the auspices of European Student Relief in 1923. In 'The Editor's Travel Diary' in *The Student World,* he wrote:

The peculiar tragedy of Germany is not its suffering, which is not so great as that of some of its European neighbours, and, as I told the students, not in the same category as that of China. It lies rather in the isolation of that suffering, and the total uncertainty of its outcome.

Robert saw it as a first priority to combat this isolation, short-sightedly perpetuated by the policies of occupation authorities, which only compounded the propagandist educational background of the Nazi period. On this occasion, he was able to tell a student meeting of a thousand at the university of Tübingen that, a few days before, the Executive Committee of World Student Relief had determined to pursue contacts with books and material aid for German students. Under trial and persecution, church and SCM in Germany had found themselves driven closer together, leading to the creation of 'student congregations' with a considerable increase in numbers in consequence.

Reminiscing in the summer of 1991, Marie-Jeanne remembers the tenacity and humour with which Robert tackled the conquest of the Berlin blockade. After sitting for hours in drizzle, 'perched furtively upon a luggage barrow', having been turned off the train in the Russian zone, Robert suddenly said 'Guess what day this is ... April Fools' Day!'

As a Swiss Marie-Jeanne had no visa for the British sector, so Robert told her, 'Don't open your mouth and look as British as you can!'

They elected to try to track down Hanns Lilje, now Bishop of Hanover within the British sector. After a delighted reunion amongst the rubble, he used his expertise to find them a plane to Berlin. Indeed, the following plane was shot at, so they acquired an escort of fighters for the return journey.

Marie-Jeanne describes what their visit meant to the pastors and students, some just returned from prison camps, encouraged to share openly their past experiences, their fears for the future, and able at last to discover what had been happening in the world outside Germany. It was on such occasions as these that Robert most clearly displayed that combination of imagination and understanding which underlay his ability to relate to others. She emphasises how an intuitive grasp of a situation in all its complexity was then followed by practical ideas for its alleviation: 'A rare combination of charity and honesty which produced a stimulating and constructive challenge to those he was dealing with. Never intimidated.'

In Robert's Travel Diary he wrote movingly of his visit to Czechoslovakia after the barriers had come down in 1948:

As I heard how new huts had been opened on the camp site in memory of Jaroslav Simsa and Jaruslav Valenta, those two Christian leaders who

*lost their lives in Nazi concentration camps, I was moved by a sudden
memory. Just ten years ago I landed on this same airfield a few weeks
after the Munich crisis, three days later than I had promised. Everyone
had given up meeting me, save Simsa, who said quite simply: 'I knew
that you would come.' Ten years ago I had wondered if Czechoslovakia
could ever again have complete confidence in Western Europe, but I had
rejoiced in the loyalty of my friends. The consequences of the betrayal
of 1938 are part of the painful reality of today, but the courage and
loyalty and faith, which Simsa proved in his life and death, remain and
I came away grateful to God for the present, and future, contribution
of Czechoslovakia to the life of the Federation.*

As Robert moved about the shattered post-war world, always
in close contact with countries and continents, even when they
proved impossible to visit, he was acutely aware of the political
ambiguities of the times. He saw the demand for a Christian realism, sometimes alongside, sometimes over against Marxist idealism,
secular cynicism or disillusionment and despair. Within the new
World Federation of Democratic Youth and the World Federation
of Students (later the International Union of Students), there began
a struggle between different understandings of democracy, accompanied by varied attempts at co-operation, which demanded a
sophistication of approach difficult for the average student to master.
Some retreated into a narrowly personal concern, expressed either
in religious or materialistic terms. Robert wrote in a 1946 editorial:

*What is the bearing of Christian hope upon the political frustration in
which younger people feel themselves enmeshed, or the dogmatic positions
they accept in escaping from it? One answer ... is that political life is
not really the business of a Christian, who must concentrate on saving
his own soul alive, and rescuing, where he can, the souls of others.
Another answer ... is that political problems are all soluble, if only
an atmosphere of goodwill can be generated and a limited number of keen
Christians placed in strategic public positions. Both these temptations
must be resisted by a <u>Student</u> Christian Movement .... Now is the time
for our student groups to think out what they believe as Christians, to
resist all sweeping judgments, to avoid all meaningless slogans, to reject
all specious invitations to comradeship, while refusing to be cut off from*

their fellows by externally imposed barriers, and above all, to believe in
God in Whose purposes rests the future of mankind.

Again, in 1948, as the Cold War intensified:

We are fully aware that some readers think that we should avoid the
discussion of politics in the pages of The Student World, *and indeed in*
the Federation itself. This argument is based on the truth that as
Christians we are primarily concerned with the Gospel. Now let us freely
admit that political discussion may be a way of escaping from the
demands of Jesus Christ upon our lives. But so indeed may be worship
and Bible study and evangelism. Any human activity may provide
an excuse for avoiding a face to face encounter with our Lord ....
When we try to keep our politics separate from our religion, and out of
our movements, it usually means that our political opinions will not stand
the full light of the Gospel upon them .... We know now, or we ought
to know, that the interaction of different forms of power makes policy.
We influence the future more by the food we eat, and the freedom on
which we insist, than by the opinions we pronounce or the advice we
offer to public men. We are caught in the machinery of power and it is
there that we must act as Christians. Any separation of our faith and
worship from this entanglement of our lives is like creating pleasant
gardens round a factory without concern as to whether it is manufacturing
for the essential needs of men or for their destruction.

There were now new tensions in the life of the Federation
either to be resolved or to be held in balance. In 1947, in an issue
on democracy in the Federation, Robert wrote:

The sharpest test of the next year or two ... will not be whether student
opinion is being expressed in the Federation, but whether the Feder-
ation can avoid all imputation of being Western or European. This will
not be achieved so much by running about the world to find new meeting
places or by constantly bringing new groups of students together, but by
ensuring that, wherever and however the Federation meets, it thinks in
world *Christian categories.*

On a 1949 theme on assessing reconstruction, he wrote:

> *And now as we ... look ... around at the suffering and enmity of the*
> *present, and ahead at a future which seems already to cast sombre shadows,*
> *it seems unwise to speak of reconstruction at all. Had we not better*
> *confine ourselves to that more temporary, less ambitious, word – relief?*

The extent and the urgency of student need in Europe, China and South East Asia compelled Robert to give a great deal of time to the intricacies of fund-raising and co-operation within the ISS. It was the very existence of World Student Relief, with its methods of mutual assistance and student self-help, that did more to alleviate the situation than the material aid it was able to give in the way of food, clothing, books, paper, mimeograph machines and laboratory equipment.

As war-time restrictions eased, and before new cold war prohibitions could comprehensively take their place, world-wide meetings became possible and necessary. The first major event in 1947 was the World Conference of Christian Youth in Oslo. Robert had been chairman of the planning committee since December 1945. He was instrumental in the formation and development of the World Christian Youth Commission, which included the World's YMCA and YWCA, the WSCF, the new Youth Department of the WCC, and the long established World Council of Christian Education and Sunday School Association – all very different in origin and ambience. His whole approach to such complicated diplomatic exercises is summed up in his exhortation: 'It might simply be a convenient organisational arrangement to avoid friction or it might become a new beginning in the total work for Christ amongst the youth of the world.' [3]

Ans thus it proved to be at Oslo, as 1300 young people had their first experience of ecumenical fellowship and challenge. The young Philip Potter, later to become General Secretary of the WCC, then newly-arrived from the Jamaican SCM (itself the product of Robert's activities from Toronto), tells of first meeting him on this occasion. He watched Robert deal with a succession of crises, the first being 'the confrontation between the Indonesian delegates and the Dutch'. Then the presence of Germans caused the King of Norway to refuse to participate in any way. Philip Potter commented:

I thought of the person of Barnabas in the Acts of the Apostles, the one who always encouraged and enabled people ... his quiet way of going round, you know, looking as though nothing was happening, while trying to do the right thing... there were a lot of sores that were still open and those of us who came from ... the third world were in a very militant mood ... and in that atmosphere ... in one of his devotional addresses [Robert] *said, 'It is by thy mercy that we are not consumed' ... this has stuck in my mind ever since.*[4]

In 1948 a British 'Quadrennial' was held at Westminster under the title 'Summons to Christian Obedience': it drew a membership of 2,000 – 200 from overseas. Living with the nuclear threat was to become such an integral part of life during the cold war period that it is not easy for subsequent generations to imagine the atmosphere of dread and guilt which was engendered in Christian circles by the use of atomic weapons against Japan at the close of the war. It was this that lay behind the 'sense of hopelessness' which was addressed on this occasion by speakers such as Hanns Lilje and Reinhold Niebuhr, and which gave birth in the next decade to a new theology of Christian hope in which Jurgen Moltmann, once a British prisoner of war, played a significant part.

At the same time, many remember that their concern for international affairs dates from the Westminster event. This concern, however, was now set in an even wider world context with less specific concentration on the Indian situation which had sometimes pre-occupied the pre-war British SCM.

In the same year two other major assemblies occurred within the Federation family: the Triennial Conference of the Indian SCM in Madras, and the North American Student Volunteer Conference at Lawrence, Kansas. From the North American Conference report, Robert quoted the following in his Travel Diary: 'We thought to claim the unoccupied frontiers of the world, but we found that Christ was seeking to claim the occupied frontiers of our hearts and wills.'

In these post-war years Robert worked with a superb team of colleagues such as John Coleman, Suzanne de Dietrich, Marie-Jeanne de Haller, Eric Duncan, Francis House, T Z Koo, Philippe Maury[5], Andreas Schanke[6], M M Thomas[7], Winburn T Thomas[8], and K H Ting. Robert had great confidence in them and they in him. Eric Duncan, in particular, marvels at the capacity he had to concentrate utterly on the subject in hand whilst keeping numerous 'other balls in the air': 'He was never content just to carry on; his eyes were always also looking to see what wasn't being done, what needed to be done. The best chief in the world.'[9]

Recalling Robert's style of leadership, Marie-Jeanne observes that the one characteristic with which he had no patience was pomposity and 'people who thought they were important. He never thought he was important – what he had to do was very important, but *he* was not important. He really trained us with that in mind – not that he was a hundred per cent successful with any of us! He would not allow us to take ourselves seriously no matter what, but he certainly made us work hard and enjoy it'.

Again, in conflict and controversy: 'Because of his simple genuine faith and lack of fear he could not be used – a great strength in tricky situations. In those his great sense of humour was a blessing.'

She adds:

It sounds really like too much praise! Yet it is true ... the man had weaknesses like everyone else ... his absolute lack of musical sense. Hearing him leading the singing of 'The Lord is my shepherd' was absolute agony, totally out of tune, and with such enthusiasm![10]

Robert responded to his staff's preoccupations by creating opportunities for their development without prescribing results, an Abrahamic approach at some variance with certain modern types of management theory. An example of this was the Federation's contribution to the discussion on the nature of the university. A study was initiated by a short book edited by John Coleman, followed by a consultation at Bossey and an issue of *The Student World*, and continued by a collaborative series of meetings and publications. The emphasis was on the university appreciated for its own sake, not merely as a context for other activities. In his editorial to the relevant issue, Robert wrote:

No longer is it possible to isolate students from their environment and to consider them as young men and women conveniently grouped for purposes of Christian evangelism and education .... The character of the university has such a profound effect upon its members, and basically such a non-religious effect, that the Christian faith appears irrelevant. The prophets are in danger of crying in a very real wilderness, and the presentation of the Christian Gospel runs the risk, not only of looking ridiculous, which is its glory, but of being ridiculous, which is its disgrace.

In a most important sense, this approach involved the working out in practice of an evolving theology of the relationship between church and society, which gives due significance to the proper place of human community in the scheme of creation and redemption. Appropriately, Robert quoted in its defence the words of that seminal, if insufficiently appreciated, thinker, J H Oldham:

What has become essential is the ministry of creative love, the translation of the power of faith into the creating of human community in all kinds of groupings in the secular life.

Such a theological approach has the particular virtue of escaping the excessive individualism which has – oddly unscripturally – characterised much protestant thinking.

In several such areas, Robert saw his colleagues rather than himself as taking the lead. Their later perception, however, is overwhelmingly of his personal contribution both in empowering them and in responding to people and events. As each issue of *The Student World* took up a current theme, so his editorial conveyed the essence of the Federation's concern with that theme. His involvement was so total that when he was struggling to adjust to his WCC job in 1950, he was to write to Dorothy, 'I suppose the real problem is that I had so thoroughly identified myself with the SCM and the WSCF that I can't fall in love again!'

We find an official tribute to his work as General Secretary contained in the report on the life of the WSCF, 1946–1949, prepared for the 1949 General Committee in Whitby, Canada:

The quality and nature of the contribution which Robert Mackie has made can perhaps be suggested in the phrase 'pastor extraordinary to the student world' .... With deep understanding, with a clear sense of the vocation of the Movement and with rare Mackian humour, he has shepherded each staff member .... Under his wise leadership people have found themselves doing what they believed impossible. Under his touch, instead of producing constant and increasing friction, the diversity of back-grounds and experience has been made to yield vast richness for the for-warding of a common Christian task .... In spite of disclaiming any particular gifts in administration Robert has shown administration to be an art .... [11]

His time as an officer with the Federation drew to its close with the first Assembly of the World Council of Churches at Amsterdam in 1948, an event so long deferred. Philip Potter describes him as Visser 't Hooft's 'right-hand man' on that significant occasion. [12]

Robert had a particular involvement with the participation of the Youth Department; its delegation broke new ground in a prophetic way by insisting on equal numbers of men and women. At the open-air youth rally, considerable sensitivity was needed to introduce a German speaker in a Netherlands so recently occupied; the German was, however, Niemöller [13], himself recently released from prison.

At the same time, however, through the crowded days and nights, Robert was also wrestling with Visser 't Hooft's offer of the job of an Associate General Secretary linked to the Director-ship of the Department of Inter-Church Aid. His hesitations were many – both about the dimensions of the position and also about his own suitability. The desire to return to his roots in Scotland was still strong; his close Scottish friends such as Professor Willie Tindal of New College, Edinburgh, suggested that he could leave his return no longer if he were still to find congenial work there. Thus Robert was bewildered and a little sad that, in the home of Edinburgh 1910 and much ecumenical and missionary enthusi-asm, there seemed to be little understanding of his own clear sense of vocation as a Church of Scotland minister in a world context. In a letter to Dorothy from Amsterdam he quotes from that out-standing world churchman, Professor John Baillie [14] (about to become one of the Presidents of the WCC), on his eventual decision to stay in Geneva: 'John Baillie says, "It is a pity you are not coming back to Scotland" – with no idea that I represent Scotland in the WCC. I am a churchless man.'

Of his advisers in general, Robert continued: 'Reinie [Neibuhr] has been the most human. He says I must go in and make the show work.'

Notes to Chapter 9

1 WSCF Archives, Ecumenical Centre Library, Geneva.
2 *The Student World*, 4th Quarter 1946.
3 WSCF Archives.
4 Interview between Philip Potter and William Perkins (WCC staff), 8.7.1988.
5 French resistance leader, later Robert's successor as General Secretary of the WSCF.
6 Later Dean of Hamar, Norway.
7 Later Director of the Christian Institute for the Study of Religion and Society, Bangalore, and Chairman of the WCC Central Committee.
8 Later Principal of Chiengmai Theological Seminary, Thailand.
9 Interview with Eric Duncan, July 1991, Stirling.
10 Marie-Jeanne interview and letter, 14.8.1993.
11 WSCF Archives.
12 Philip Potter interview.
13 Submarine commander in the First World War, minister of the Protestant Church in Westphalia, anti-Nazi supporter of the Confessing Church, a president of the WCC.
14 Professor at New College, Edinburgh, leading theological teacher and writer.

CHAPTER 10

Pastor Extraordinary

EVENTS were to prove that Robert's fears about the nature of the position he was offered at the WCC were well-founded, but this was not necessarily anyone's fault. The times and circumstances were unique and prognosis difficult. Robert was concerned that the supportive role of Associate General Secretary should not be subverted from the start by being combined with sole responsibility for the Department of Reconstruction and Inter-Church Aid; no one knew better than he how the aftermath of war had confirmed the centrality and escalated the overwhelming demands of the latter.

Already in 1948, 67 people, nearly half the WCC staff, worked in that Department. In a letter from Amsterdam dated 3 September to Visser 't Hooft, Robert clarified his attitude: first, he suggested a trial year on both sides, and drew attention to certain commitments he had undertaken for a year or so to ISS and World Student Relief as Chairman of the WSCF – typically suggesting a salary reduction as a consequence. He continued:

> *I understand that, if I receive an invitation, it will be to become an Associate General Secretary, carrying out such functions as may be agreed upon from time to time. I further understand that I should be entrusted with certain staff relationships in Geneva, and with certain administrative responsibilities. I see no difficulty there, except that I believe it ought to be quite clear that I am not the Administrative Secretary requested .... I should like it to be understood that I have neither the skill, nor the inclination, for a job which would consist entirely of office administration.*

Robert was very happy, however, that he should have some sort of advisory involvement with the Youth Department. Then he raised his main concern:

> *I am extremely uncertain about any relationship I might have to the Reconstruction Department* .... *Is it possible to carry this relationship along with the others mentioned above?* .... *In that case my work must be largely as the chairman of a staff team* .... *I see the point of attempting to integrate the work in the total work of the Council, and I should be prepared to attempt this, but only if all concerned – in USA and Britain as well as in Europe – knew that I was not a full time director, but had other responsibilities.*

He then suggested some necessary re-organisation of personnel in the Department if the 'new experiment' was to have any chance of working. He concluded:

> *If I have overstated the case, or if you do not feel that problem can be tackled drastically, then I feel that I should not be asked to be a part time director but that a full time director, able to handle all the details and all the staff relationships, should be found.*[1]

Whatever Visser 't Hooft's personal response to this, or the intentions of the appointing committee, Robert's desired balance between the overall concerns of an Associate General Secretary and the oversight of an Inter-Church Aid Department was not in fact achieved. Wim let it be clearly understood that Robert was 'in charge' if he himself were out of Geneva, but did not sufficiently adjust his own self-sufficient and idiosyncratic working methods to enable this to happen satisfactorily. On one such occasion Robert wrote to him in New York from Geneva, saying how much more 'use' he could have been as a 'stand in' if the original arrangements had been adhered to.

In a letter to Dorothy from the Second WCC General Assembly at Evanston in 1954, Robert confessed: 'It is impossible to share Wim's burdens because I never know what he is going to do next.' This facet of the General Secretary's character in no way undermined their mutual trust and affection; it did, however, cause

Robert constant concern at what he saw as his own failure to sustain 'two quite incompatible responsibilities'.

Whilst about his Department's business, Robert tried to represent the totality of the World Council's concerns, wherever and whenever possible: for example, in a memo to his colleagues before a Greek visit: 'I do not fancy myself as a Study or Faith and Order man, but if any of you have got some rather simple instruction that you would like me to carry about in my head please let me have it.'[2]

Certainly the burden of the full time Directorship of the Inter-Church Aid Department was Robert's from the start . Indeed, in 1952 Visser 't Hooft suggested that Robert should be proposed as Deputy General Secretary at the Second General Assembly. By that stage, however, Robert had several objections to the idea – not least that it would be inappropriate to have two churchmen from the same 'Reformed' tradition at the centre of the WCC staff. (Then, as now, issues over the significance of the representation of denomination, geography, gender, age and ecclesiological status tended in ecumenical circles, perhaps unavoidably, to complicate the selection of the best person for the job.) It is probable, however, that the widespread dismay which greeted his departure from the WCC in 1955 arose partly from the perception that he had, in fact, functioned as 'acting General Secretary', in the words of Frederick Nolde, the only other Associate General Secretary appointed at Amsterdam to be reappointed at the second Assembly[3]

In 1948 Robert was well aware that he inherited at the Department a situation of crisis – only in part financial – as the emphasis of the work moved from the needs of the immediate post-war period to a longer-term strategy. Although there had indeed been co-operation between churches on matters of aid for three decades, (much of it through the Central Bureau for Relief of the Evangelical Churches of Europe begun in 1922), the setting up of the WCC, in preparation and in fact, had brought a new theological understanding of the centrality of such service; it was now seen to be of the very nature of the church itself and, therefore, of the relationship of the churches to one another and to secular society. In his valuable account of the history of European Inter-Church Aid, *Tears and Rejoicing*,[4] Pieter Bouman speaks of it as belonging 'to the life blood of the ecumenical movement'. Visser 't Hooft located the origin of this new perspective in the 1937 'Life and Work' Oxford Conference, operating under the prophetic guidance of J H Oldham[5]. The conviction behind the setting up of the WCC's Department of Reconstruction and Church Aid was that member churches, now irrevocably committed to one another, must pursue their task of service together – an ecumenical *diaconia*. At the very least, this would be the most effective use of resources in the context of an overall assessment of needs and priorities. Moreover, only such a unified approach could meet genuinely Christian criteria for authentic witness.

The theory was, indeed, understood and accepted by church representatives on the WCC, but the practice proved much more difficult. First, there was a major task of integration and co-ordination of different bodies and agencies, including the International Missionary Council. More intransigent in the long run was the phenomenon of resurgent denominationalism which accompanied the revival of interest in ecclesiology. The development of world confessional organisations had – and has – a tendency to undermine a joint ecumenical approach; thus the growth of bilateral church aid was the chief source of the financial aspect of the crisis. Insufficient and insecure funding also lay behind the rate of staff turnover, with its attendant waste of energy and expertise.

The programme of activities was very wide: refugee care, re-union and resettlement of displaced people, individual health aid including a rest and holiday centre in Locarno, the exchange of fraternal workers, the provision of theological scholarships across countries and confessions, an Ecumenical Loan Fund and a work camp programme – administered after 1950 by the WCC Youth Committee.

Robert was never an empire-builder and, not infrequently, ventures which had their origin in the ICA Department found their further development in other divisions of the WCC. Another example was the place and understanding of the laity. Jean Fraser, for some years a Youth Department colleague, writes of Robert's 'inventiveness in finding a home in your Department for the wilder schemes of the Youth Department ... you have again and again saved the kitten from having its tail trodden on'.

This, however, is not the context in which to tell the story of the work in all its personal and moving detail, a story which can be found in the more general histories of these years. Here it may be sufficient to say that Visser 't Hooft in his *Memoirs* concluded: 'Only with regard to inter-church aid is our record perhaps somewhat comparable to that of the early church.'

The spirit in which all these activities should be undertaken was agreed from the beginning and frequently reiterated, not least by Robert himself. It was one of equal partnership, a solidarity in which the characteristic of 'receiver' or 'donor' was of merely random local and temporary significance. The present writer recalls testimony to the reality of this attitude in the tributes of West German church leaders, who themselves exhibited the harvest of such a sowing in their outstandingly non-directive financial support of eastern and southern European churches during the period of the Cold War.

Otto Dibelius, Bishop of the Evangelical Lutheran Church of Prussia and a WCC President, wrote in 1955:

> *Of all ... churches probably none has come to realise what you have made your World Council division mean to the needy and homeless more beneficially than has felt our Evangelical Church in Germany during the first after-war decade. <u>Inter-church aid</u> and <u>service</u> to <u>refugees</u> those words have become signs of a mutual covenant and a common rededication to the Divine Healer of all our wounds. Whether one member suffers, all members suffer with it; or one member be honoured, all the members rejoice. So our Aid is more than an emergency operation; it is of the very essence of the Church Universal.*

From Hamburg comes an addendum:

> *When once the history of the ecumenical movement has been written, then the name of Robert C Mackie will have a brilliance all its own ... [with] a very special ring in the German congregations in both East and West.*[6]

In the immediate post-war years, under the Directorate of Hutchinson Cockburn, another Scot, ecumenical National

Reconstruction Committees had been set up in 'receiving' countries such as Poland, Germany and Greece, and similar bodies in 'donor' countries such as the USA, France and Britain. These were asked to co-ordinate needs or possible resources respectively so that the Department could be in a position to make judgements on priorities.

With equity in mind, 'donors' were requested, wherever possible, not to 'earmark' offers for particular purposes, and 'receivers' to record and report gifts which had arrived from other sources.[7] This sort of minimal ecumenical discipline proved very difficult to achieve, particularly as the WCC had neither the wish nor the authority to do more than advise and persuade. As a result, it proved necessary during Robert's time to move to a more project-based programme. In his first report in *The Ecumenical Review* in 1949 Robert wrote: 'We must be ruled by consecrated intelligence rather than by superficial emotion.'

The WCC Central Committee, meeting in Chichester in the same year, had approved the substitution of the concept of a 'continuing service' for that of 'reconstruction' – 'a permanent obligation of a World Council of Churches which seeks to be true to its name.' The Department's title was consequently changed to 'Inter-Church Aid and Refugee Service', the latter to reflect the primacy of demand.[8] In the same article, Robert concluded:

> *Thousands of people in Europe only know the 'World Church' or the 'Ecumenical Movement' through aid which has come to them from their fellow Christians. Deeds have spoken louder than reports and resolutions. Historically speaking the crowning achievement of the Church's post-war work of reconstruction may be found to have been in an increased understanding of other people, and a stronger sense of Christian solidarity. These are the things that make for peace. That is why co-operation is a key word in Inter-Church Aid. Any failure on the part of a national inter-church committee to be fair in its allocations; any tendency of a church outside Europe to help its co-religionists out of all proportion to their comparative needs; any attempt to encourage confessional loyalty through the distribution of aid; any refusal to establish proper clearances, and above all any spirit of competition, cuts*

at the heart of Inter-Church Aid and saps the foundation of the World Council of Churches .... Such co-operation is perfectly compatible with direct relationships between churches. Churches wish to help, and to be helped, as churches. It would be contrary to the whole spirit of the World Council of Churches to hinder that good impulse. But we must not fall into the ever present temptation of confessional selfishness. There are countries and churches – specifically, Eastern European countries and Orthodox churches – which are liable to be grievously neglected unless the ecumenical setting of all our inter-church relationships is maintained. Only in this way shall we be certain that the work of Inter-Church Aid is building up, not only individual churches, but the whole Church of Christ in Europe.

Regrettably, the warning still appears to be needed in each succeeding generation.

Forward-planning assumed a greater importance. From an ICA Consultation in Geneva in October 1950, as the Cold War intensified, Robert wrote:

The future of Europe is once again at stake. What matters is that life should be renewed from its deepest sources. It is here that the role of the Church in Europe is most clearly seen. The Church is not there simply to conserve, or to protect, but to enable men and communities to be born anew ... this work has not simply been a matter of transferring funds, or supplying food and clothing to meet necessities. Inter-Church Aid has been a distinctive factor in binding the Churches of Europe together and in linking them with Churches outside Europe. The result of the giving and receiving of gifts has not been merely an improvement of material conditions, or even temporary encouragement. Inter-Church Aid has had a deeper significance. Men and women have experienced the reality of the life of the Church of Jesus Christ through the acts of Christian fellowship .... Today the Churches must be ready to meet new situations created by expulsions of people from one country to another, or by the disastrous results of civil war, or by the artificial political and economic barriers between East and West which become daily more formidable.[9]

Out of such thinking, and through other inspired leadership over

Robert Mackie in the uniform of the 2nd Lt Highland Light Infantry, 1918.

With his father, James Mackie, on holiday at Fortingal, 1935.

At Swanwick Conference in the late 1930s:
(left to right) Bishop Neville Talbot, Archbishop William Temple
and SCM staff members Roy Whitehorn, Robert, Behrens and Alan Booth.

With the WSCF staff in Geneva, 1946:
(left to right) Eric Duncan, John Galevan, Robert, unknown, Philippe Maury,
Marie-Jeanne de Haller and Suzanne de Dietrich.

With three of the preceding General Secretaries of the WSCF, Geneva 1946:
(left to right) Robert, Visser 't Hooft, Henri-Louis Henriod
and John R. Mott.

As General Secretary of the WSCF,
at his desk in 13 rue Calvin, Geneva, 1946/7.
Photograph taken by Leo Zander.

Dorothy Mackie, *circa* 1946.

Outside an 'Emergency Church' in Germany, 1949.

Robert in Glasgow Doctor of Divinity robes, 1948.

With Dorothy and Steven, Geneva, 1951.

Chairing the Beirut Conference on refugees in the Middle East in the 1950s.

Three WSCF Chairmen, May 1953:
(left to right) Visser 't Hooft, John R Mott and Robert.

With Dorothy, visiting Iona Cathedral in June 1957.

With Steven outside the British Museum, 1954.

The blessing of Scottish Churches' House, Dunblane in 1960:
with Metropolitan Juhanon, Ian Fraser in work clothes
and Robert 'merging into the background'.

Robert in Kingston,
Canada, 1975.

Steven speaking at the WSCF
Conference, Edinburgh –
the Centenary Celebration, 1995.

the next few years, the Conference of European Churches was to be established.

Within the context of the Department's general concerns, experience disclosed specific problem areas calling for a flexibility of response: the position of Protestant minority churches in Latin countries was one; and that of Eastern European churches in general was another. The Orthodox Churches, both East and West, had peculiar difficulties. Robert was given special responsibility for relations with small Orthodox Churches and communities in exile, a role which entailed a good deal of individual assistance. He was equally concerned, however, for the needs of the great national Orthodox churches, most of whom had been prevented, in these early years, from becoming members of the WCC. To the 1950 Central Committee in Toronto he said: 'The Department watches to see that projects on behalf of the Orthodox in Europe, are not forgotten, and that the needs of "silent churches" are made known.' A special recommendation was issued:

> *The Central Committee recognizes that there are Churches in Europe and in particular Orthodox Churches, which do not have sister Churches of the same communion able to help them. It, therefore, asks all contributing Churches to set aside and place at the disposal of the Department some portion of their giving for this ecumenical service across confessional lines.*[10]

Recognition of his efforts in these areas is vividly apparent in the letters he received when he left the WCC in 1955: officially, for instance, from Bishop German of the Serbian Orthodox, and Archbishop Athenagoras of the Greek Orthodox, from the Russian Orthodox in Geneva and Paris, and on a more personal level from the Rector of the Romanian Orthodox Church in New York who writes:

> *I know and you know it also, that I could not have been able to do as much for the Romanian Student Christian Movement and for the Romanian Refugees, without you help. On the other hand, when I managed to escape from Romania, you were the first man to whom I appealed. I shall never forget your straightforwardness and discretion.*

Your way of doing things does not apply only to me, personally; but to all other Romanian Refugees and Orthodox from all countries behind the "Iron Curtain". As a minister of Christ you have been the main channel through which the parable of the Good Samaritan was applied on a very large scale. In the whole history of Christianity, for the first time, Christian Churches of the West have been wonderful in doing as much as they could in helping their fellow brethren, who lost everything but their Faith in God and in their fellow-men. Words cannot express our real feelings .... If you think you will retire from this kind of work, you have so wonderfully achieved, you are mistaken old boy. We need not only your knowledge and experience. We need your wit and deep understanding of Christian problems and human nature. We need your modesty and simple directness and especially your masterful way of conducting meetings and discussions. These qualities made you very dear to all of us and especially to the Orthodox, who would not have hesitated to make you a <u>Patriarch</u>, except that would have meant sacrificing your beloved wife Dorothy, who already has made so many sacrifices for you and for all of us.[11]

Whilst deprecating the exaggerated claims on his own behalf, and also on behalf of the Western churches, Robert took singular pleasure in the unlikely picture conjured up by the suggestion of the Patriarchy, and also in the honorary doctorate that he was awarded by the college of St Sergius in Paris.

From 1951, in response to events in Korea and the Middle East, and in gratitude for the generosity to churches in Europe from those outside – ('I have only to report that ... new gifts for the life of the Church in Europe have come ... from a union church in Siam, from a hill church in Formosa, and from a Methodist congregation in Haiti'[12]) – Departmental strategy began to develop an inter-continental perspective.

The ratification of such a strategy was on the agenda of the Second WCC Assembly. It was developed in close co-operation with the International Missionary Council, which had hitherto acted on behalf of the churches in non-European areas; such co-operation, involving a great deal of committee work, was facilitated by Robert's life-long commitment to missionary concerns. Indeed, the fact that he did not accept employment with the

International Missionary Council itself on the various occasions when he was approached to do so, was largely the result of particularities of time and circumstance. Frequently in demand as chairman/mediator at consultations between the WCC and the IMC, his letters reveal a determination 'to speak "straight" to both sides', as well as a rueful acceptance that 'trust' had to be won again on every occasion from new staff.[13] It is out of such patient concern (by many others, such as Lesslie Newbigin, as well as Robert), and the strong views of Federation-trained church leaders from all parts of the world, that the successful integration of the IMC into the WCC was finally achieved at the Third WCC Assembly at New Delhi in 1961.

It is important to emphasise that neither Robert nor any other church leader saw the churches' contribution to the relief of human misery as other than a drop in the ocean of the world's need, a need which demanded for its satisfaction the resources and will of the world community as a whole. At every point, therefore, they co-operated with the relevant governmental and international institutions. The peculiar emphasis of the specifically Christian approach is strikingly given in a report of Robert's words in an issue of *Agape*, the news sheet of the Youth Department:

> *To give should be to confer the power to give; the fire kindled by love should light other fires; new links should be added to the chain of gratitude which goes back through the ages to the first response to the love of God in Christ, when the shepherds and the kings brought their gifts. 'Beloved, if God so loved us, we ought also to love one another'.*[14]

Robert remained Director of the ICA until late 1955 and then became Chairman of the Department until 1961. In his commendation of a joint WCC/IMC strategy in Asia and Africa after Evanston, he stressed the necessity for taking very seriously society's structural problems in an era of rapid transition: '... it is folly to concentrate on ameliorating the worst effects of social change, and not to enable the churches to see the part they must play within that process, so alarming in its rapidity and so overwhelming in its results.'[15]

He welcomed, therefore, closer co-operation with the Division of International Affairs in a joint study on this theme. From the start he appreciated the economic and political sophistication required in the administration of aid programmes on a global scale: he warned 'that relief action may often be damaging, leading to further pauperisation, unless it is wisely handled'.[16]

There is something salutary in the fact that this most understanding but clear-sighted of men ended his 1954 Evanston report in the *Ecumenical Review* on a severe note:

> *Love is a quality which must be shared. And it is in short supply because Christians so readily turn inward on themselves. The household of faith calls for our special care, not because it is a family which should survive, even though others perish, but because only through it can the world be reached. And what we have to give the world is not our casual aid nor our surplus commodities, but, in and through them, this same love of God which we cannot receive unless we pass it on. 'Do not be deceived,' St Paul wrote, 'God is not mocked, whatever a man sows, that he will also reap'.*

Whatever his doubts about his own capacities, Robert always remained convinced of the importance of the work of Inter-Church Aid and he brought to it all his resources of commitment, diplomacy, patience and humour. With a firm discretion he helped to transform several precarious national situations as in Britain with the emergence of Christian Aid from a previous ICA base.

The tributes paid to Robert when he left in 1955[17] are almost overwhelming in their range and depth of feeling. From some there is shock and even anger that he has been allowed to resign when the need for his beneficent presence is so great:

> *We shall still have a World Council, of a sort, after you depart, but it will no longer be the one we have known. We shall miss your mellowed wisdom, your infinite good-nature, your skill in presenting and discussing weighty matters in committee or larger company*
>
> ~ Douglas Horton, Harvard Divinity School ~

> *This greeting will probably be different from any other that you receive.*

Without hesitation, I tell you that I do not want to write it. I rebel against the occasion which calls for it.

~ Frederick Nolde ~

I had not yet succeeded in completely reconciling myself to your departure. I feel deeply that some arrangement should be worked out which would assure beyond any doubt your continuing close association with the top level of the Ecumenical Movement ... it is not easy, indeed not possible, to put in words the admiration and gratitude which one feels for all you have given.

~ Pitney Van Dusen, President,
Union Theological Seminary, New York ~

I feel as if I were losing my own right arm and as if the Council were crippled still more sadly. If you really insist that the time has come you can at least have the deep satisfaction of having established the Division in a magnificent way. I shall always remember the pitiful condition of the program of Inter-Church Aid when you came into it. When I compare those days with the present I am full of rejoicing and thankfulness.

~ Samuel Cavert[18], New York ~

From every part of the world the tributes came – from Beirut, Djakarta, Finland, India, Kenya, Korea, Rio de Janeiro, Yugoslavia ... the list lengthens. There are many famous names – Bishop Bell of Chichester, Bishop Berggrav of Oslo, Bishop Hanns Lilje of Hanover, D T Niles of Ceylon, Visser 't Hooft ('I consider it one of the greatest blessings of my life that I have been allowed to have you as colleague') – and many quite unknown, such as an office neighbour whose total message was: 'From now on what a pity – I do not need to hurry in the morning as I won't meet you any more! I am so sorry.' A postscript on one runs, 'Also our cleaner, Mme Rossier, regrets deeply your departure'.

A colleague, Nils Ehrenstrom, submerged under a 'flood' of documents, confessed that he *always* read those that issued from Robert's own pen:

For here I have felt, with singular personal immediacy, the living heart-

beat of the blessed movement which we have been called to serve ... it has been a constant inspiration and challenge to follow what you have been accomplishing so superbly, like a twentieth-century St Paul, in drawing the Churches together in the fellowship of caring for the needs of the poor among the saints.

Others maintained that both his writing and his preaching had been determinative of their vocation within the church:

I shall never forget your preaching of God's Word, through which I was helped in the deepest way. I pray that in the future your service may more and more be in the pulpit, where with gentleness and wisdom and courage and reverence you made it possible for me to repent of my sins, and to receive the pardon of God in Jesus Christ. It is a wonderful thing for any man to win so much love in his lifetime.

The attitude of Robert's field staff might well be summed up in the words of one: 'Your loyalty to your colleagues and your disinterested concern for their welfare give a tremendous sense of security ....'; a perception echoed in Hans-Ruedi Weber's words, 'This precious gift of yours, this "charisma" of giving confidence, we shall miss most ....'

Another writes: 'More than most of us realize, you have served as a kind of ecumenical cement, to hold together the galaxy of primates and prima donnas who adorn the World Council fellowship. You have done much to humanize the rarefied atmosphere ... your greatest contribution has been to help provide the ecumenical movement with a heart.'

Youth camp leaders attributed to Robert the 'human quality ... most happy surprise' of the WCC leadership: 'God had really sent you to the kingdom "for a time like this" ....'

The young Robert in Scotland in the 1920s, doubtful of his financial abilities, would have been amazed to know that Henry Leiper of the American Friends of the World Council would one day write of him: 'most certainly no-one could have extracted so much money and still have left doors open for welcome return year after year!'

Some comforted themselves with a conviction that his legacy

would remain – 'You are leaving, but not your spirit' from the Bishop of Melita; and, from Charles Arbuthnot[19] ...

Months ago, when I first heard of your intention to turn over your work in Geneva and return to Scotland, I was shocked almost beyond words. Why, you had become Inter-Church Aid! In the intervening time I have come to see how you have prepared the rest of us better than I had realised. You leave us a way of working which is yours but which will ever be a resource when our own ways would have failed.

It is not perhaps surprising that many have been disappointed to find that Robert Mackie's name is not even mentioned in the entry on Inter-Church Aid in the *Dictionary of the Ecumenical Movement* published by the WCC in 1991.

'For seven years, you, with Dr W A Visser 't Hooft, have been the World Council of Churches,' wrote American Methodist Bishop Oxnam. The existence of such sentiments was, indeed, one of the reasons behind Robert's decision to initiate his own departure. From the time when he followed the veteran Tissington Tatlow at the British SCM, through his experience of joining 'the apostolic succession' of Mott and 't Hooft in the WSCF, to his dealing with a range of established world organisations struggling to adapt to changing circumstances, Robert had developed a deep concern over the damage that could be done by the best intentioned leaders staying on too long. 'People have no notion of the importance of change at the right time.'[20] On the other hand, it may be that he underestimated just how differently his style of leadership was regarded. He had a horror of anything in the nature of a 'cult of personality' – 'I get a certain following amongst church leaders,' he wrote to Dorothy, 'but the problem is how to make "precise" use of it.' And, on another occasion: 'It is the trouble of being a person to whom no-one objects.'

It is revealing to read, in the intimacy of his letters, how he reacted to one event: 'Humanly speaking it was rather a success. A group of tired people responded to my informal style of preaching. I am embarrassed by constant expressions of thanks! God alone knows whether he used me, or could use me.'[21]

Certainly he felt a lack of advice during the critical period when he was making his decision to leave the WCC. Bishop Oxnam, writing of his 'clarity ... a spirit so winsome as to be convincing ... good humour ... patience ... tolerance ... the song that has always been in your heart', adds the perception of 'the fact you have kept your personal problems to yourself so that none of us really had opportunity to share in burdens that all of us must of necessity carry.'

In March 1953 Robert wrote to Dorothy:

I don't know if I am wise to be so categorical about my future in the WCC. I just felt I had to be categorical <u>at some point</u>, or I should lose my personality in a world I don't feel to be mine. I <u>hope</u> I am not fighting against God. The WCC is surely not the Kingdom. I don't mean to retire from that! I try to be open to God's leading .... I don't was to be running away.

In October Robert returns to the subject: 'I'm sure it was right not just to drift on as an essential prop to Wim in the WCC. I get awful nightmares about my work and about my doing the wrong thing.' And, a month later from New York: 'Clearly no one here can conceive of why one ever gives up a job if it is a good one – especially with no other in prospect!'

He was quite clear that his decision to move did not spring from personal dissatisfaction, and acted quickly to dispel a rumour to this effect. He remained doubtful, however, of his achievements as Wim's assistant, following him around on American visits:

I pick up odd functions of my own .... At least I can try to work on the fringes .... Wim has a queer unconscious way of omitting me from conversation .... He has seen and done everything imaginable, and I get involved in the ends of what he has done with people.

In the midst of reconciling groups and personalities, Robert writes:

[Wim] remains so essentially indifferent to all that and so devoted to the cause that I love him for it. Yet he is getting more and more isolated as he becomes the WCC idol. I don't know how anyone is going to get

*alongside him. It needs friendship – and an ability and interest in
public life that I lack. The future General Secretariat worries me a lot
… the other thing that worries me is deserting the machine and the
responsibilities – the terrifying responsibilities, which the whole refugee
work has entailed.*

The resolution to his second concern lay in the appointment of
a good successor to the Directorship of the Department in the
person of Leslie Cooke, and in Robert's own acceptance of the role
of chairman for a period of years. His personal preference would
have been to accept the suggestion of such a position in a quite
different department, but as ever the needs of the work took
priority in his mind.

It has to be admitted that Robert had never been wholly at
ease in the environment of official church leaders with its greater
formality and bureaucracy (necessary as he judged this often to
be), as churches for the first time engaged with each other as
churches. Early on he found 'a great need for patience and compromise' at a Central Committee meeting 'curiously lacking in
these qualities'. The letters contain occasional phrases which are
indications of his feeling: 'I am more than ever convinced that I am
a misfit in this kind of ecclesiastical/political world'; and latterly …

*I must leave not only because there is need for new leadership and not
too many British and more brains than I have, but because [also] I am
always terrified that in this public life I may suddenly do harm to the
things I love …. Only another week of battle – battle on the part of
a stuff-shirted General! I laugh at myself now and feel better.*

On a visit to Scotland near the beginning of his time at the
World Council, Robert tells Dorothy, 'I think being in Scotland is
bad for me, in that it makes me regard this stage as a prolonged
interim period to which I don't belong …. I have a feeling here of
being utterly empty and lost. But perhaps God speaks through
empty lost people.'

It did not help that he felt, in spite of his own loyalty and
affection, that his own Church of Scotland did not really see in him
any kind of representative or ambassador; its national conciliar

structures, whatever their other virtues, make it difficult for the Church to place and own the service of one whose vocation has led to wider and unexplored ways. This being the case, it is ironic that Robert himself found considerable satisfaction, if only local appreciation, in adding to his work-load by becoming pastor to the Scots congregation in Geneva. It is the only context, at this time, in which he speaks of actually 'enjoying' his work.

The Scots Kirk in Geneva likes to trace its origin to the English speaking congregation of 1555-1560, of which John Knox was a minister for some three years. After a three hundred year gap, in 1867, there developed an almost unbroken tradition of summer chaplaincies to serve the needs of Scots visitors, largely under the inspiration of a Genevan Pastor, Charles Martin, who had studied in Scotland and become a historian of the earlier period. After the founding of the League of Nations and associated international organisations based on Geneva in the 1920s, a more permanent nucleus developed and was served by longer and more continuous chaplains until the appointment of a full-time Church of Scotland minister in the person of Thomas Watt from 1926 to 1935. The life, activities and organisation of the congregation were by then sufficiently developed for it to survive a return to a series of temporary chaplaincies.

From his first arrival in Geneva, apart from the interruption for the Toronto years, Robert became frequent preacher, adviser, pastor and friend both to chaplains and a congregation increased by the presence of the WCC and other Christian international agencies. The constantly changing staff of these always included a proportion of English-speaking adherents to the Reformed tradition. True to his ecumenical credentials, however, it was Robert who initiated and achieved, with the full support of the Church of Scotland, an official fraternal Association with the National Protestant Church of Geneva. From 1951 until 1955 he was indeed the official minister, part-time, of the Scots Kirk which, when he left, was ready, as a member of the Church of Scotland's Presbytery of Europe, to receive a full-time ministry. It currently provides a good example of evolution from a chaplaincy to ex-patriates, which is largely irrelevant to the changing demographic and ecumenical climate, to an international, ecumenical English-speaking congregation fulfilling a specific contemporary need. It may yet pioneer a greater measure of integration within the Geneva church scene.[22]

Supporting Robert at the Scots Kirk involved Dorothy in considerable hospitality, in spite of her declining health, and the correspondence reveals how much unobtrusive pastoral work she also had to undertake amongst his Departmental staff during his frequent absences on its business – a staff which, through him, had come to see itself as more 'a family' than a 'team'. As the years passed, his marriage and Steven remained his sustenance and pleasure; Dorothy's letters eased the burdens of his travels and he was continuously articulate in his expressions of affection, always counting the days until their reunion. 'I cling to the belief that, if I could live a stretch of life in small compass with you beside me, I could make my own soul yet.' He valued her advice beyond all others, which is, of course, why he wrote to her in such detail about his work and feelings. In 1951 from Beirut he acknowledges, 'I am so grateful for your companionship – especially at this bit of my life, which I find the most difficult of all.'

The place of Steven in his life assumed a continually developing significance. Already in 1947 he had written, 'Steven seems to me the one point of permanence. His growing mind and spirit belong to the present *and* the future.' Robert gained considerable satisfaction from Steven's progress at Edinburgh University and in the early evidence of his independence of mind. His marriage to a fellow student, Annebeth Gunning from the Netherlands, and the birth of a first grandson, James, in 1954, was a source of great delight. 'We have got this new family starting now and we have a new sort of life to begin.' As a corollary he remarked, 'I can get up no interest at all in my own future.'

In this context he saw his role, with Dorothy, as providing a Scottish base for the extended family, all the more necessary when Steven and Annebeth went to Madurai in India where Steven had been appointed Chaplain to the American College.[23] Robert was keenly aware of the part played in his own life by 'Croftlands', the family home in Biggar, where his mother had died at the end of 1950. He had taken a lively interest in its refurbishing, in the garden and its tree planting, in the neighbours and the local churches. It was to 'Croftlands', therefore, that Dorothy and Robert finally returned from Geneva. Before this, however, they made an extended visit to the young couple in India, which enabled them to develop an informed picture of their life and work.

In July 1956 Robert was able to write to them of Jamie from Croftlands, 'I think of him often in the garden here. We have kept a lot of ridiculous odds and ends that he will be happy to play with. But sometimes when I think of him it is really Steven I see running down the path after *his* Grandad!' [24]

Perhaps the last word on Robert's period with the WCC might come from that most knowledgeable source, Philip Potter, who by 1955 had returned from work in Haiti to the Youth Department:

[Robert] *was absolutely indispensable to Wim and to the Council as a whole. He was the man who took care of staff and brought his Scottish common sense and administrative skill to keep the Council going. Wim was the master mind, the great synthesizer, and the man who had ideas. Very often Robert would put Wim's grand things into a sentence or two. I know that Robert was deeply respected in all that he did in Inter-Church Aid during those years ... he was a household name in Europe ... nobody rushed into the press about Robert because in Europe you rush to the press about what somebody writes or some great utterance which meant Wim got the press but Robert didn't. But when people spoke about somebody who came to their help, it was about Robert.*

More surprisingly, Philip replied to the question, 'You would never call Robert much of a radical, would you?' with 'Oh, Robert was. He didn't make a big noise about it'. [25]

Notes to Chapter 10

1   WCC Archives, Ecumenical Centre Library, Geneva.
2   Ibid.
3   First Director of the WCC's Commission of the Churches on International Affairs, consultant to the United Nations on Human Rights.
4   Doctoral dissertation, University Theological Faculty, Brussels, 1983.

5   Letter from Visser 't Hooft, 22.4.1983: Mackie Papers, Edinburgh.
6   Tributes to Robert on leaving the WCC, 1955: ibid.
7   WCC Archives.
8   Ibid.
9   Ibid.
10   Ibid.
11   Ibid.
12   Ibid.
13   Letters from Robert to Dorothy: Mackie Papers.
14   WCC Archives.
15   Ibid.
16   Ibid.
17   Mackie Papers.
18   Prominent American ecumenist, WCC staff member in New York.
19   European representative of the Presbyterian Church of the USA.
20   Letter from Robert to Dorothy, 18.8.1953: Mackie Papers.
21   Letters from Robert to Dorothy, Spring 1953: ibid.
22   Notes on the Church of Scotland in Geneva, William A Mackay, Geneva, 1990: ibid.
23   After three years in India, Steven followed his father as a staff member of the British SCM (1953-63) and of the WCC (1964-/4). He then became a lecturer in Practical Theology and Christian Ethics at the University of St Andrews (1974-93).
24   Letters from Robert to Steven: ibid.
25   Philip Potter interview.

CHAPTER 11

The Home Stretch

'HOW proud Scotland should be of her son Robert Mackie,' wrote a young Scots minister, George Buchanan, in 1955; 'and how grateful should her Church be to one who has served her so superbly and given such a grand witness to her and to the Master whom she serves.' At the time, and later, it did seem to some, from their own positions of prominence in various parts of the world, that Robert left Geneva to vanish into an obscurity from which he emerged four times a year to convene meetings of the Department of Inter-Church Aid. He was, they felt, an example of 'the prophet ... not without honour, save in his own country'. Such a judgement, however, proceeds from a perspective on life and vocation very far from Robert's own.

What happened in reality was that he began, and continued for thirty years, to exercise a very similar kind of leadership in ecumenical affairs, but within the confines of one small country – his own. This was an arena which yielded little reward or status because it was peripheral to any of the existing structures of church or society – but these were never considerations in Robert's mind.

He accepted the part-time position of 'Adviser for Ecumenical Work in Scotland' with the Scottish Churches' Ecumenical Committee which was made up of the official representatives of the churches, in collaboration with the Scottish Churches' Ecumenical Association, which was a membership organisation for groups and individual enthusiasts.[1] There was a small honorarium attached, which of course bore no relationship to his previous salary. Robert, however, had always been extremely careful about his personal financial affairs, saving where possible from small family legacies, concerned only to be in a position to take care of his family and to maintain his freedom to undertake the work which most needed doing. To Steven in India he wrote in May 1956: 'It has been a wonderful experience for me to be wanted by these younger men, who have been waiting for me.'[2] He was, moreover, supported in his decision by old friends such as Willie Tindal and Ralph Morton.[3]

There is no doubt that the Scottish churches in the 1950s were in need of an imaginative, experienced, ecumenical leader such as Robert, even if they did not altogether deserve him (although the hard working individual ecumenists undoubtedly did).

The basic historical division of the Reformation had been followed in succeeding centuries by the results of separatist tendencies within presbyterianism itself, compounded by receptivity to other denominational groupings of diverse origin. Either because or in spite of this sectarian legacy, twentieth century Scotland had, however, provided an early home to ecumenism, particularly with a missionary perspective, as in 'Edinburgh 1910'. The first Scottish Council of Churches had been created in 1924 on the base of the Missionary Campaign Continuation Committee born of that great event; it had eight members, the Church of Scotland, the United Free Church, the Scottish Episcopal Church, the Congregational and the Baptist Unions of Scotland, the Wesleyan and the Primitive Methodists, the Reformed Presbyterian Church, with the Original Secession Church joining later. The variety of forms taken by the ecumenical process from 1924 to 1964 is clearly traced in Mabel Small's *Growing Together*, published by the Scottish Council of Churches, with a foreword by Robert.

Scottish churches had played a leading part in the setting up of the British Council of Churches in 1942, providing its first General Secretary in the person of Robert's good friend, Archie Craig. By the time of the first WCC Assembly at Amsterdam in 1948, however, ecumenical co-operation in Scotland seemed to be more fruitful outside than inside the original Scottish Council of Churches, and it agreed in March 1949 to dissolve and be replaced by a new Scottish Churches' Ecumenical Committee. Arguably, however, the dynamic was provided by its partner, the Scottish Churches' Ecumenical Association, which co-ordinated individuals and groups. Robert worked with and through both, and with and through a wide variety of other organisations.

The main agent of ecumenical outreach at this time was the 'Tell Scotland' movement and Robert became Chairman of its Executive. This movement had recently sponsored a 'Billy Graham' campaign, but it also involved those who were uneasy with such evangelistic methods; the newest initiative to come under the 'Tell Scotland' umbrella was a 'Kirk Week' to take place in Aberdeen in August 1957 – Robert was forthwith given the task of chairing the planning committee. Other agencies which used him were the Scottish Ecumenical Youth Council, Christian Aid, the Week of Prayer for Christian Unity, the gradually developing local councils of churches, and the Dollarbeg Group. The latter had arisen in response to a WCC Study Department project on the life and work of women in the churches and had led to a series of most lively conferences; these were centred on themes of particular concern to the laity such as the significance of work, communism and secularism.

All these bodies were full of life and vigour, but there was also a fair measure of organisational confusion and some conflict in style and leadership. No wonder he wrote to Steven:

My chief worry now is whether I can hold it all down! …. Tell Scotland is stimulating, but seems in a difficult moment. My coming as chairman of Kirk Week … is regarded as a sort of 'deus ex machina'! But I don't feel at all deified – only lost in a maze of names, movements and conflicting views of evangelism! I should never have chosen to plan this thing so quickly …. But I must take it as it comes.[4]

One of his unavoidable commitments in a full summer in 1956 was the chairing of a second crucial consultation in Beirut on the Arab refugee situation in the Middle East; the first had been in 1951. These were co-operative ventures undertaken by the Department of Inter-Church Aid and Refugee Service and the International Missionary Council, and also involved other voluntary organisations and the United Nations World Refugee Agency (UNWRA). For this reason, and even more for the intractable nature of the problem itself, they proved events of much political and ecclesiastical complexity. With no political solution in sight, the plight of over a million displaced people continued to make demands that could barely be met in spite of the efforts of UNWRA, the churches and others. The festering bitterness amongst the Palestinians was rightly judged in the report to be a breeding ground for future conflict – and so it proved with the emergence of the Palestine Liberation Organisation (PLO). Robert was never to face a more demanding chairmanship than this.[5]

Back in Scotland, the most urgent task was the planning of the Aberdeen Kirk Week. The concept of a 'Kirk Week' owed something to the German post-war Kirchentag, an integral part of an extraordinary lay Christian movement which had its roots in the German church experience of the disastrous 1930s and 40s. Naturally Robert had been familiar with the German development throughout; indeed he had already promised to be involved with the 1956 Kirchentag, where he had a brief reunion with Reinold Niebuhr and Niemöller. From it he wrote:

> *So many people is always tiring but the crowd was so good natured and the meetings so interesting that I enjoyed it … a fascinating discussion on the Church and Politics … which gave a sense of participation though there were 12,000 people in <u>that</u> hall!*[6]

(Total numbers at a Kirchentag were frequently around 50,000 with up to half a million from both East and West Germany at great open air services.) It is impossible not to admire how Robert retained his capacity to respond on such occasions – even to a theme which, in his own life, was proving burdensome.

The Kirk Week concept had, however, more specifically Scottish origins as well. Many were ill at ease with the mass rally on the American pattern as the most appropriate evangelistic method for the churches in the 1950s. This led to a sustained search for alternative ways of outreach to an increasingly secularised society. This was combined with a conviction that the church could fulfil its vocation within that society only in so far as the whole of the membership understood and accepted its vocation: this would involve a process of continuing adult Christian education for both ministers and people. Some even claimed that the Bible and theology had become 'prisoners' to the cleric and the academic. The 'priesthood of all believers' had, of course, been dear to the hearts of many church reformers down the centuries, only to be constantly subverted by the ecclesiastically convenient alternative of the clericalising of further selected lay groups – such as the eldership in the Church of Scotland. The first Kirk Week, therefore, would be a genuinely pioneering event, and one very much after Robert's own heart.

He inherited a planning structure of some inadequacy: he confided to Steven,

> *On Tuesday I went to a Kirk Week Executive. I find it rather nerve-wracking because it is made up of such busy ministers giving it a fraction of their time. It <u>ought</u> to be a layman's committee, but I have no time, nor means, of creating this at this stage. I feel that everything is in the air still .... Yesterday I made out a Draft Plan of Organisation, which I hope to get into action .... I hope I can manage to help them. It will take a lot of wisdom – and prayer. At least I have got them to arrange a sort of Retreat for the Committee .... We have to get a group really <u>under</u> the event .... I must get people to see that this is an enormous job, which needs action, and yet not be alarmist*

And later:

> *... I am fighting for lay leadership as against clerical push. Tell Scotland is still run by keen clergy. There is no Reinold* [von Thadden, founder of the Kirchentag] *.... I told the Synod that Presbyterianism seemed to have frozen its laity in an ecclesiastical system and I think that's about right. But Ian* [Mactaggart] *and G. F. M.* [George Macleod] *encourage me to press for lay leaders for my hundred groups.*[7]

Robert was delighted when a young minister, Colin Day, was seconded for six months in February 1957 to undertake the organisation of Kirk Week.

To this variegated Scottish scene, then, Robert brought all his resources of experience, patience and good humour. As ever, he listened, learned, animated and inspired, able to provide both a British and a world context for policy and action. 'All our worship, fellowship and activity as Christians in Scotland,' he wrote at the time, 'are simply a small fraction which we can see of the total work of God in Christ throughout the world. We need a national focus in order to play our part in a divine and human enterprise beyond our imagining. If our ecumenical co-operation loses that vision, it loses its animating power.'[8]

At the same time Robert accepted numerous preaching engagements of all kinds: St Giles, the Usher Hall ('quite an ordeal for me'), University chapels, large city churches, country villages ('small high Scottish pulpits with a sprinkling of folks at the back'), 'a Church parade for 2500 BB [Boys' Brigade] boys in the St Andrew's Hall' (Glasgow); he did this partly because, as in Geneva, 'the church' for him was always local as well as world embracing, partly because he felt it was necessary for the work he had chosen to do that he should get to know as many younger churchmen and women as possible. In his letters he is full of praise for the parish ministers (and their wives) he came across as he pursued this course – ministers and wives such as Ian and Margaret Fraser in Rosyth.

Agreeing to act as Honorary President of Edinburgh SCM, Robert was disappointed, if not surprised, to find the ecumenical situation extraordinarily similar to the one in 1926 – an SCM with an 'open' membership, an Evangelical Union affiliated to the Inter-Varsity Fellowship with a 'closed' membership, and a Christian Union in the middle. The new element was the development of denominational chaplains and consequently denominational societies, largely the result of the SCM's own post-war re-emphasis on the centrality of the church. This had brought about a decline in numbers in the SCM itself, although there was considerable co-operation between the 'open' groups, most chaplains having had their own nurture within the SCM in their student days. A new 'Christian Community' umbrella under the University Chaplain, James Blackie, attempted to supply a reconciling mechanism.

All in all, he told Steven in November 1956, 'I *think* I am usefully – if not *gainfully* – employed!"

But the next year, in a letter to Dorothy, he writes: 'This is a far more difficult life than having one job. I only hope it is of some use to others.' From meetings in Geneva: 'It is so difficult to explain

to people who ask, "What is your post now Dr Mackie?"' On a
similar occasion: 'The idea of an odd job man is unthinkable.'
Again: 'It is a queer broken career now – all in bits – unrelated.' On
the other hand: 'I am so glad that all the student people are asking
for my co-operation. It is really exciting …. I still prefer to work
with the young'; and, 'it is a fascinating job or series of jobs'.

The path Robert had chosen demanded a quite remarkable
combination of vision, clarity of mind, tenacity of purpose and
personal humility. So convinced was he of the need for freedom to
adhere to the strictest ecumenical priorities, that he even gave
up after a while the only element of his work that attracted any
remuneration – that of part-time 'Ecumenical Adviser'. Writing to
Dorothy on the subject, he ruminated: 'there is no place for someone who stands behind efforts in Scotland – or at least it is better
to do that as an entirely private individual!' And: 'I have to try to
find the centre again and again. But the real centre is God himself,
and *you* help me more than anything else to keep in touch with
Him.'

Throughout his marriage, Robert's closeness to Dorothy had
been developed by means of a constancy of correspondence, all the
more remarkable on his side for the busyness of his days. After
their return to Scotland they both took great pleasure in adjusting
Croftlands to their needs, at the same time retaining its original
character. 'Granny's old clock remains unchanged where I put it in
1926 on the mantlepiece,' he wrote to Steven in Madurai. 'The
place is very pretty now with pinks of different kinds, foxgloves
stalking through the rockery with impudent dignity, peonies,
violas, catmint, poppies, irises …. And always there are the hills
and the cattle walking up them in the evening and the cries of
sheep.' And again: 'The trees are your age, for Father brought
them back from a roadside at Grantown!'

It was not difficult in Biggar to get good and congenial help in
both house and garden – for so long cherished from afar. The
help was very necessary, not only because of the travel still associated
with Robert's commitments – although these gradually decreased
in distance and extent. The major factor, however, was the slow but
steady deterioration of Dorothy's health in spite of close medical
care and varieties of treatment, some in hospital. The arthritis and

associated conditions gave her much pain and, over the years, proved increasingly disabling. Indeed Robert's decision to care for her at home in Croftlands was only made possible by the long and devoted service of his housekeeper, Mrs Fraser, who stayed with him until his own death in 1984. Emphatically non-church-going, she said of him in 1991: 'He was the same with everyone – he didn't overdo it' – the kind of cryptic Scots comment Robert would have appreciated.

As early as 1957 he had written to Steven of his mother's condition, 'I have the problem of preventing her becoming a sort of hermit invalid .... So I think next winter I must plan to be more at home. But then there will not be the stimulus I bring from seeing people – and so it goes.'

A last French holiday together took place in Nice at Easter in the same year; as Dorothy could walk so little, every day he hired the same 'Victoria' horse carriage to tour the environs, a reminder of his grandmother's Helensburgh establishment in his boyhood.

Robert remained chairman of the WCC's Inter-Church Aid Department until 1962 and also accepted the chair of the British Council of Churches' International Department for a similar period in order to facilitate the co-ordination between the different levels of ecumenical activity. His Scottish friends were divided in their advice as to whether he should take on the extra BCC burden, as indeed he was in his own mind, but he was concerned to maintain the Scottish input at the British level. He told Steven, 'it is difficult to get a layman who is not politically marked for the job .... A letter from Wim saying that it was difficult to make the right contacts *today* between BCC and WCC clinched the matter.'

This responsibility soon assumed a graver aspect with the Suez crisis in late 1956. This gave rise to several emergency meetings in London, Paris and Geneva as the British churches responded with urgency and concern to the British government's actions. Steven in India was anxious for first hand news – both of Suez and of the short-lived Hungarian revolution. From Geneva, Robert wrote:

We then turned to Hungary. You must understand that up to a week ago the Hungarian churches were on the phone to Wim with rejoicing.

*Even the SCM ... came into existence for three days! Then the tide
turned, and silence came. It is a frightful tragedy. The good churchmen
... had been reinstated. What will now be their fate? ICA had got into
action ... supplies got through. Now we are deeply involved with
the refugees ... we sent out messages to the member churches about
Hungary and the Middle East refugees.*

The next month he was able to make a four-day visit to
Hungary on behalf of the WCC; on such a confidential occasion
his decades of contacts earned him trust from more than one
generation, and he was able to keep Visser 't Hooft informed
from within. Of the situation he found, he wrote: 'Europe still
has its Confessing Church.'

It was during this period that the BCC's International Department's work included a great deal of discussion on the subject of
nuclear disarmament, a subject over which Christians disagreed
sometimes with more passion and dogmatic conviction than
charity or open-mindedness. Robert chaired with his customary
skill, but was uneasy in such an atmosphere. 'Older men thanked
me at the end for impartiality and realism .... But I find this realm
very barren and uncongenial,' he wrote to Dorothy.

The Aberdeen Kirk Week, when it finally happened in August
1957, proved a most stimulating occasion; Robert had succeeded in
involving both Martin Niemöller and Hans-Ruedi Weber, WCC
Laity Secretary, in the preparatory meetings. Over a thousand
registered, but there was also every attempt to make it a city-wide
occasion with associated normal local Sunday services at start and
finish, and open plenary sessions. The Lord Provost hosted a civic
service and a civic lunch, and the whole was presided over by Sir
Thomas Taylor, Principal of the University (and President of the
Scottish Churches' Ecumenical Association). Of this first national
lay event Robert wrote: 'We learned ... that Christian fellowship
was not a sentimental cushion on which you fell back when you
were tired, but a dynamic force capable of changing your whole
outlook, and providing an energy you did not previously possess
....'; and: 'This understanding of lay responsibility in the affairs
of the world ... came to be known as "The Kirk Week Line".' [9]

As the result of the 1957 Committee's initiative, a financial appeal made it possible for Colin Day to be appointed full-time 'Tell Scotland Secretary for the Laity' in 1958 and to undertake the preparation of another Kirk Week in Dundee in 1959. This was followed in the course of time by Kirk Weeks in Ayr and Perth.

Over the years Robert proved himself willing to take on a leadership or a subsidiary role in innovative projects of many kinds where he thought he could be of use. He was a key figure, for example, in the imaginative reconstruction of several small eighteenth century houses in Dunblane, given by the Friends of the Cathedral in order to create Scottish Churches' House as a visible symbol of unity; it is still jointly owned and greatly valued as the base for ecumenical co-operation. In a letter to a friend, Ian Fraser gives a graphic account of how Robert went about recruiting him as the first Warden:

> *We sat down together and he told us that the seven churches in Scotland had come to the point where they were prepared to have a building in common as their base, and that a row of eighteenth century houses in Dunblane might be saved and used for the purpose as a 'house of the churches'. Someone was needed to head this up on the spot. With his usual honesty he indicated the situation to be faced: 'At present we have no money for restoring the buildings, although we do hope to raise enough. We also have no money to appoint someone to head this up although we would launch an appeal to raise it. What would you think of taking this on?' .... Margaret ... said simply 'That's for us!' .... So, in 1960 I took on a six month's assistantship at the Cathedral to provide for our maintenance and used the time for work camps in the summer and for starting the work on the House by the autumn .... others had strong reservations about appointing such wild cards as Margaret and myself, but Robert persisted and won.*

The work camps discovered in the rising ground behind the house an ancient vaulted stone building, the sole remains of the mediaeval Archdeacon's house; this they transformed into a chapel of lasting significance.

The year 1960 was the Jubilee Year of 'Edinburgh 1910' and the influence of Robert can clearly be seen in the siting in St Andrews that summer of the WCC Central Committee, whose members were brought to Dunblane Cathedral to give their blessing to the enterprise; the Metropolitan Juhanon of the Mar Thoma Church of South India unveiled the 'Oikoumene' symbol in the wall of the house. Robert made sure that Ian and the members of the work camp were present throughout in their working clothes – in such imaginative ways is the universality of the church demonstrated.

Many distinguished churchmen supported the creation of Scottish Churches' House as a place of healing for the divided churches – 'here, on this ancient, sacred site .... the very heart of Scotland,' as the Earl of Wemyss put it at the opening ceremony. Robert gave particular credit to Nevile Davidson, the convener of the Scottish Churches' Ecumenical Committee. Ian Fraser, however, insists that Robert himself did most of the work of promotion and raising money between meetings, merging into the background on official occasions.

At another celebratory event in 1960, (also attended by the Central Committee) – a service in St Giles – Robert stood by the Queen Mother, always known for her church interests, to introduce the array of colourful world church figures.

His Geneva colleague, Madeleine Barot, formerly of CIMADE, once said of him, 'We French like to talk about things, but it was Robert who saw what had to be done'. Such an opportunity arose with the designation of Livingston New Town as 'an area of ecumenical experiment', the result of suggestions made at the Scottish Faith and Order Conference at St Andrews in 1963. A new type of 'ecumenical parish' was to be created in the new town, with a jointly-owned building for worship, and Robert became Chairman of the Livingston Committee, guiding it through the early difficult years when there were prolonged and tortuous relationships with regional church structures. James Maitland, first Church of Scotland member of the Livingston team, recalls Robert's laughing remark – 'It's a life sentence!'

Something of the speed of this development may be deduced from the fact that the label 'experiment' was not abandoned by the General Assembly of the Church of Scotland until the 1990s, by which time England had produced around 500 similar parishes.

In the preface to Mabel Small's account of Scottish ecumenical activity, Robert wrote:

Co-operation between Churches does not come naturally. That sounds out of keeping with their character and objectives. But it is true. A national Church ... is a self-sufficient body, acknowledging 'One Holy Catholic and Apostolic Church', but organising its life as if no other Christian body existed. Ecumenical thinking and acting calls for conscious effort, and because it means going outside [the] normal machinery of the Church's business, such effort is seldom strongly continuous. The churches may be growing together, but the process is one of fits and starts, of genuine enthusiasm checked repeatedly by slackening of interest. Anyone who cares about Christian Unity must be prepared for hard knocks, and sudden unexpected opportunities of advance.

During the 1960s Dorothy became more and more dependent on Robert's care and affection, expressed through letters when he was absent. When writing from Geneva he constantly rehearses the pleasures of their life there together in the detail of walks through remembered streets, meals in familiar restaurants, visits to old friends and that most evocative of Genevan images – primroses in the grass. 'Geneva pulls my heart strings as ever. We left more of ourselves here than anywhere else, Toronto and London not excepted.' Concern for Dorothy radiates from his pages. He worried over the extent to which it was right for him to travel. In August 1958 he writes from an Austrian ICA meeting:

I shall come back from Athens – paying the difference myself – if you find it too difficult. I do love you so much, and yet for me not to travel would build walls around our life which need not yet be there. So many people ask for you .... You are still very much part of this wider fellowship. Indeed the ecumenical world is still our home. I find myself more widely welcomed, more surrounded by friendship, here than anywhere in Scotland. Also I am quite clear that my greatest usefulness is still in this milieu .... I think one of my functions is to keep the whole business of human relations alive in the midst of machinery.

Again: 'I always feel we serve the church together.' Family and friends, including Steven and Annebeth when they were in Britain, supported Dorothy with their regular visits, especially when Robert was away.

He still practised the self-disciplined lifestyle he developed over the years, combining travel, meetings, hours in preparation and correspondence, with physical exercise, prayer, Bible study, general reading and the art of personal, listening conversation. At the Nyborg WCC Central Committee in 1958, for example, this regimen included sea bathes before breakfast, where he appears to have been joined on a markedly less regular basis by friends such as John Baillie. Few people, indeed, are as good as Robert was at keeping friendships in repair, partly through a deliberate availability even during congested conference timetables, partly through the resolute maintenance of habits of correspondence, even on occasion rising in the middle of the night to reply to a letter. His letters themselves bear testimony to the methodical nature of his reading habits, from Bonhoeffer's *Ethics* ... 'getting *moments* of illumination', to George Macleod's latest ... 'a strange mixture of the incisive and the elusive'. Once again he established systems and routines of work, but now with only a little part-time local secretarial help.

Robert's relationship with Visser 't Hooft remained affectionate and close; Robert continued, however, to be concerned about a certain kind of isolation in which the other man worked. He wrote to Dorothy from Nyborg: 'obviously the good man welcomes my arrival. He has never found an intimate colleague. That moves me and troubles me.' He was also acutely sensitive to his relationship as chairman of ICA to his successor as Director, Leslie Cooke, trying always to be available but not intrusive. Of this he wrote on the same occasion: 'I think perhaps my *being here* does no harm.' He was determined never to take advantage of his previous position, giving, for example, a required report to the Executive, then immediately withdrawing ... 'I know my place'.

It was on this occasion, in the privacy of a letter, that Robert mourned the tedium consequent on poor chairmanship of a committee: 'X gets prosier and prosier! We discuss and discuss ... the appropriate text was "a dog returning to its own vomit".' Aware, from experience, of the conflicting demands on resources of time, money and people, he attributed a serious value to efficiency.

Throughout the late fifties and early sixties the Dollarbeg consultations and SCEA conferences continued, with Robert

normally involved in planning, speaking or writing. The two-day
SCEA event in November 1957 in Edinburgh's Assembly Hall,
for example, drew over 600 on the theme 'Scotland Faces the
World's Need'. Their last conference in 1964, with even larger
numbers, centred on 'Mission', to celebrate the final integration
of the WCC and the IMC, and included speakers of the calibre of
Lesslie Newbigin and K A Busia, Methodist layman, eminent
sociologist and later Prime Minister of Ghana.

Robert's expertise with meetings became increasingly recognised. Writing from one of the last ICA Committees convened by
him in November 1960, he remarks how strange it is to be
chairing once again in the American context. 'Several *younger*
Americans have come up and asked me questions on method!
They have all expressed pleasure at seeing the thing done in a
wholly new way! I have been trying to explain how to handle an
ecumenical and international group ....' He still remained worried
that 'as usual, I shall have seemed to be too dominant', whereas
Lesslie Newbigin once claimed that no one could so thoroughly
'efface themselves' in committee as Robert. Philip Potter, third
General Secretary of the WCC from 1972 to 1984 and recognised
by Robert as a young black Caribbean minister of promise at Oslo
in 1947, has said of him:

> *I learned leadership more from Robert than from Wim. I learned from
> Wim ways of handling a meeting in terms of resolutions and how to
> arrange political strategies, but how good humouredly to conduct a
> meeting I learned that from Robert, which means that Robert had a
> sense of intercultural sensitivity. He didn't have the linguistic abilities
> of Wim but he had inner sensitivity.*[10]

Archie Craig, in his 'no nonsense' way, just insisted that Robert was
'the world's best chairman'.

As a 'consultant' at the New Delhi WCC Assembly at the end
of 1961, Robert writes: 'It is queer being so idle .... Everyone
expects me to know everything and I am simply a spare part.'
Present on that occasion at a discussion for theological teachers,
he reports wryly the comment of a young delegate:

*'There was a paper about this long ago that Robert ...... wrote –
what was his name?' And everyone began to laugh! I feel queerly
superannuated when so many people ask 'What do you do now?'
.... I don't quite belong anywhere now. Just a man who knows too
many people. I am a part of history, a part they quite liked!*

On the other hand, 'I like the contact with people who still regard
me as an elder brother.'

Acutely aware, after Amsterdam and Evanston, of the administrative pit-falls of Assembly organisation, and of the additional
complications in the Indian context, Robert is full of admiration
for the success of so much of the New Delhi event; he is delighted,
also, by the final official accession to the WCC of the Russian
Orthodox Church. At the start, however, he had once more
reiterated his continuing concern on such occasions, unavoidable as it had to be if they were to achieve their purpose: 'I think
the pain of this experience will be that it does not belong to
India at all ....'[11]

Accompanying him to a high level reception hosted by the
Indian Government, Robin Barbour[12] tells how Robert recalled
similar functions in pre-independence days: 'The only difference
is that the water flows like champagne,' he remarked. His current
close association with the Scottish delegation, however, introduced a further perspective and he could not avoid the conclusion:
'How provincial we are!'[13]

It is credibly reported, although the process is shrouded in
secrecy, that Robert's name at least once arose during the arcane
procedures from which emerges annually the choice of the Moderator of the General Assembly of the Church of Scotland. He
would have made a remarkably good one, not only because of his
proven ability to chair difficult and unwieldy meetings, but because
he possessed that combination of humility, humour and interest
in other people without which Moderators may, quite uninten-
tionally, prove to be a considerable liability. As neither a parish
minister, academic or conventional missionary, however, his
credentials will have seemed somewhat suspect to the average
clerical mind. There is no evidence that he was at all interested in
the matter.

Indeed, the only occasions on which Robert found lack of official Church of Scotland recognition difficult were when old colleagues at the World Council called for his experienced advice at some event, such as the closing stages of integration with the International Missionary Council which he had done so much to negotiate, only to discover that he was not to be present, not being included in his Church's delegation. He was, consequently, sometimes invited by the WCC as a consultant, but it followed that he was not then eligible for membership of subsequent committees.

It would seem, therefore, that what is perceived by some as his premature disappearance from the wider scene, arose rather from the mismatch of structures: there were and are no foolproof ways to guarantee a right balance between continuity and breadth of representation in ecumenical institutions. It was, moreover, disconcerting for him on occasion to find himself representing the Church of Scotland by default, as it were, when a designated delegate was unable to attend, for whatever reason, all the sessions.

All the while, his loyalty to his church, the Church of Scotland, was total. He became a member of one of the two Biggar churches, Gillespie Moat Park, and became friend and helper to a succession of ministers in the town – John Warnock, Hugh Davidson[14], and Cameron Mackenzie – men with quite different theological perspectives. His support could be taken for granted. He was even able to exercise his ecumenical talents on the local level as the two charges began to work increasingly and fruitfully together until they united in 1975. Moat Park itself was linked with Elsrickle, a village several miles away and John Warnock recalls that Robert quietly volunteered to take the village service on communion Sundays when the time factor made the combination difficult. He was just simply *there* for people, and, in some strange way, remained all his life the archetypical 'parish minister' – who happened never to be a parish minister.

In his involvement with his immediate community, Robert remained concerned for the welfare of the inmates of the local Loaningdale Approved School, a link with his very first adventures in leadership in the Bothwell Boys' Club. It was a great satisfaction that Loaningdale was run on humane, enlightened lines. He was, moreover, strong in his support of the David Livingstone Trust, linked not only by boyhood memory but by family ties through his brother-in-law, a grandson of the redoubtable pioneer.

In the 1960s Robert served on the Church of Scotland's Central Africa Commission during a period of some controversy. The convener was George Macleod who, at the last minute, refused to present the report to the Assembly because he wished to speak to a minority report instead. John Warnock recalls how Robert agreed to do the presentation – without notice. He defused a tense situation by beginning with 'Moderator, Fathers and Brethren, here I am in a position I don't want to be .... I feel that I am about to be slaughtered to make a Georgian holiday!'

Robert remained dissatisfied, however, with the fragmentation of the ecumenical movement in Scotland. He was aware that the Ecumenical Association, inspired by the experience of the second WCC Assembly at Evanston, had suggested in 1954 greater integration with the 'Tell Scotland' movement; this had been rejected by the latter on the grounds that it 'was concerned with interdenominational mission', whilst the former 'laid bare the divisions between denominations'. This decision had, in fact, encouraged a measure of division within churches. Mabel Small has written: 'It also perpetuated the unfortunate interpretation of 'ecumenical' as being concerned with division rather than with constructive unity, on a world scale. The two movements really needed one another ... both concerned fundamentally with the mission and unity of the Church.'

Since then the impetus of the New Delhi Assembly, the plethora of joint initiatives and events, the growth of local councils of churches, had brought a greater measure of urgency. Robert judged it imperative that 'something like a Scottish Council of Churches be set up with a central office'. So ran the memorandum presented by Robert in 1962 to a consultation drawn from all interested ecumenical organisations on the possibility of closer integration between them. Such a body should be '(a) consultative on a wide variety of issues, and (b) executive in relation to common tasks already being undertaken ... or to be initiated at a later date'.[15]

The usual and reasonable fears were expressed: possible confusion and duplication arising from churches being individually members of the British Council of Churches; the numerically overwhelming dominance of the Church of Scotland; the inhibiting of initiative and enthusiasm of individuals and groups. Of these, the first did indeed remain a perennial problem, leading eventually to the introduction of a new federal model when the BCC and the SCC were superseded by the Council of Churches in Britain and Ireland, and Action of Churches Together in Scotland in 1987 on the welcome accession of the Roman Catholic Church to full membership. The start of the Second Vatican Council in 1962 had already begun an increasing level of participation in the succeeding decades. By 1964 Robert had piloted the constitution through the necessary consultations and the new Scottish Churches' Council was set up with Ian Fraser as its first General Secretary.

Notes to Chapter 11

1   Scottish Council of Churches' Archives, Scottish Churches' House, Dunblane.
2   Mackie Papers, Edinburgh.
3   Deputy Leader of the Iona Community.
4   Mackie Papers.
5   WCC Archives, Ecumenical Centre Library, Geneva.
6   Letter from Robert to Dorothy, summer 1956: Mackie Papers.
7   Mackie Papers.
8   Scottish Council of Churches' Archives.
9   *Growing Together* by Mabel Small.
10 Philip Potter interview, 1988.
11 Letters from Robert to Dorothy, 1960: Mackie Papers.
12 Professor of New Testament at Christ's College, Aberdeen, a Moderator of the Church of Scotland and leading Scottish ecumenist.
13 Letters from Robert to Dorothy, 1960: Mackie Papers.
14 Currently a President of the Council of Churches for Britain and Ireland.
15 *Growing Together* by Mabel Small.

CHAPTER 12

From Life to Life

WHEN Dorothy died in 1974, Visser 't Hooft wrote to Robert: '... for her a liberation, for you the end of a long period of consecration of your life to caring for her. In accepting that hard task you have given to all who know you a real witness to the meaning of the faith.'[1]

During the final years of their partnership, Robert had indeed made care for Dorothy central to all his activities and had adjusted these to the inevitability of her decline. A visitor recalls how Robert would leave a series of small scuttles of coal within easy reach so that she might replenish the fire without strain. His own health suffered, but he made light of the hernia acquired from excessive lifting, and the neck collar he was compelled to wear for a period. Latterly, when confusion added to her distress, he invented a daily routine of reassurance and unreserved affection. 'Good morning, Dorothy,' he would say as she woke. 'Good morning, Robert,' she would reply. 'I love you very much.' 'I love you too.'[2] He discovered that she could enjoy the children's television programme 'Blue Peter' and they made together the toys and games demonstrated by the presenters.[3]

After 1974 the daily domestic burden lifted, to be replaced by a new loneliness. Until December 1978, however, he remained somewhat pre-occupied with his widowed elder sister, Janette, who had herself been a constant resource during the long years of nursing Dorothy. 'Having been a marvellous elder sister,' he wrote to Wim 'she now depended wholly upon me ... two years hovering between life and death ... now I miss seeing her once or twice every week and have found it curiously hard to adjust to a new kind of independence.'[4]

Visits from family and friends became more important during these years and they were also more frequent. For the first time since their marriage in 1953, Steven and Annebeth were living in Scotland, and there were regular visits, letters and phone calls, and an annual holiday together in the Lake District. Robert enjoyed getting to know his three grandsons as well. Jamie and Robin were both studying in Edinburgh and visited Croftlands from time to time, and Sandy for a short period lived with his grandfather and took the bus into Edinburgh each day to school.

Friends from Switzerland, Canada and elsewhere came to Biggar and their children (and some grandchildren) came as well, to Robert's great delight. In particular, two visits to Marie-Jeanne and John Coleman in Kingston, Ontario, brought new interests and new contacts with a younger generation of students.

In 1976 Robert was touched to be approached by the 'new look' British SCM, which had largely abandoned its national structure in favour of a community base at Wick, near Bristol. It had quarrelled with many of its 'Senior Friends' over these developments. He was asked to speak to them about Tissington Tatlow, as his name was being given to a converted building. Robert's confidential memorandum on his journey to Wick, written for concerned and sometimes alienated 'Friends', is a masterpiece of sympathetic but realistic reporting. He saw the SCM in the previous decade and a half as

> ... a legitimate and powerful expression of public Christian conscience tending to use the SCM as an auxiliary .... In the old days we used always to have a guilty conscience about evangelism. They had a guilty conscience about the state of the world, and their part in it. I believe the Holy Spirit may be at work here. What we must not do is to compare the muddled _reality_ of the present with the historic _ideal_ of the past! ....
> I had been prepared to go back for talks, but no one suggested this ....
> Now I must return to my back seat and avoid suggesting how to drive the car!

He remained, however, a constant support to local Scottish SCM staff.

In April 1979, without his knowledge, a group of Robert's oldest colleagues organised a reunion with him at Scottish Churches' House to celebrate his eightieth birthday. Aware that he would not appreciate a material gift, they asked for letters, particularly from those who could not attend; these were collected and still furnish evidence of appreciation in hindsight by a significant number of those who had themselves provided early leadership in the ecumenical movement. Three excerpts must suffice.

First, from Davis McCaughey, at the time first President of the Assembly of the Uniting Church in Australia:

> *I remember Leo Zander once asking me if I had ever thought of the question: wherein lies Robert's peculiar authority? He said: 'it is the unusual combination of the paternal and the fraternal.' He was right. To us young SCM Secretaries you were 'a father in God'. But you also were an older brother, one who stood beside us as well as one who had gone ahead and shewn the way.*

Second, from John Mackay, distinguished layman and schoolmaster:

> *I once heard it said that when Robert Mackie came into a room it was as though a light had been switched on ... all the senior members of the staff in the 1930s contributed richly ... however, there was no doubt that Robert was the producer of the play, the conductor of the orchestra, <u>primus inter pares</u>. There must be a host of people who would say as I would that their lives ever since have been different as a result of knowing him: less poverty-stricken, less shallow, less insensitive, less faithless and craven than they would otherwise have been. <u>Laus Deo</u>.*

Third, from Alan Booth, SCM General Secretary 1944-51:

> *Nothing will convince Robert of the spiritual debt we all owe him. My guess is that if we were to present him and Eric Fenn as the religious equivalent for our generation of Morecambe and Wise – each partner feeding the other with opportunities to score in accordance with his own particular talent – he might find it more acceptable, even if for us it remained an absurd travesty. How to be religious without apparently trying, how to serve God with devotion without making a profession of it, how to keep your feet on the ground and your prayers in heaven, how*

to be wholly committed and find the whole thing hilarious – it was a formidable agenda. Robert is the last person to want the ecumenical movement to be again what it once was. But a recovery of some of Robert's insights would do no harm at all to those now carrying responsibility for the ecumenical enterprise.[6]

This last judgement remains valid.

In response to Wim's birthday greetings, Robert wrote:

Your letter brought back so vividly the days when we had so much immediate contact. I always feel that I picked up from you and Suzanne, Pierre and Reinold any theology I possess! But as one gets really old it is the community of spirit of those days that speaks to one of God. I am so grateful for the thirty years 1925-1955. The 24 years since seem now an interlude. I even think of Dorothy as she was in her best years – London, Toronto and Geneva – particularly the 10 post-war years in Geneva. I always hoped I might bring back to Scotland some of what I had learnt. I don't think I was very successful! .... I have been thinking recently all over again of the God-given fact of your service to the ecumenical movement and the WCC. I cannot conceive of the WCC having that splendid start without you.[7]

The fortunate circumstance of the central location of Biggar had allowed Robert to maintain most of his Scottish committee work during the hard years of caring for Dorothy, as meetings did not involve nights away from home. Now less constrained, he was pleased in the Spring of 1979 to be asked to speak to a conference for European students at Cardiff, and 'was agreeably surprised at the evident interest in the WSCF'.

When visiting Marie-Jeanne and John Coleman in September ('they help me more than anyone'), he was still alert to any opportunity to strengthen the bonds of world fellowship and was able to have a meeting in Canada with his old friend and colleague, K H Ting, the Anglican Bishop cut off by events in China most of the time. K H Ting was able to confirm the reality of the survival and indeed growth of the 'grass roots' Chinese church, a fact which became evident to all a few years later, confounding those who had judged it wholly dependent on Western missionary leadership.

Robert reported to Wim:

[K H Ting] *himself would hope that there would only be friendly contacts from outside China and not any kind of missionary invasion .... As long as institutional organisation is not pressed – there has arisen a deep sense of being fellow Christians .... Something has happened in China which might be of real service to the World Church. God forbid that outside contacts should lead to divisions or sectarianism .... I felt it was a benediction to be in his company again.*[8]

Wim was grateful for this positive news to circulate confidentially, especially as it contradicted other more critical reports.

On his last visit to Scotland, the venerable K H Ting still spoke of Robert with admiration and affection. It was truly appropriate that it was he who led the Chinese church delegation to the WCC General Assembly at Canberra in 1991 when it was readmitted to membership, having withdrawn in 1952.

Robert wrote to Wim in 1980:

It is now twenty-five years since I left Geneva, and twenty since I lost all official contact with the World Council after New Delhi. It all seems like another world – those days when I always knew roughly what you were thinking and had the welcome task of trying to back you up. I am glad that my ecumenical effort was in those pioneering days. I get a great deal of inspiration reading One World which seems to me a most useful window into the WCC. In one sense the Council has become so much more universal than it was two decades ago. In that sense it is more ecumenical, more concerned for the whole inhabited world. I have the feeling that God has shown the churches the extent of their mission and led the Council into new channels of service. But at the same time the churches themselves have lost some of the vision and passion of the wholeness of the Church of Christ which we experienced in earlier days. Yet I am continually surprised and encouraged by the news from the WSCF ... how much more widespread is the WSCF in contacts yet how small are many of the national movements in numbers. Here in Britain the out-of-date controversy between funda-mentalists and others which I thought ... Biblical realism had ended, raises its ugly irrelevant head. Now I have an increased sense of the value and reality of the years when we were young and worked so hard through difficulties and cared so much. I thank God in every remembrance of you.[9]

It seems not inappropriate that in the year Robert died there was initiated a new inter-church process which adopted the phrase used by the Pope on his recent visit to Britain and Ireland, 'Not strangers but pilgrims'. How Robert would have rejoiced that the process came to fruition in 1987 at Swanwick, the site of so much of his youthful activity. 'The broadest assembly of British and Irish churches ever to meet … reached a common mind …. Our earnest desire is to become more fully, in His own time, the one Church of Christ, united in faith, communion, pastoral care and mission.'

As part of the same process, 'Action of Churches Together in Scotland' (ACTS) replaced the Scottish Churches' Council, making its home in Scottish Churches' House, Dunblane. In his last address to the Friends of the Scottish Churches' Council (the successor to the SCEA and soon to become the Friends of ACTS), Robert had made a suggestion: 'We need,' he said, 'an occasional national, preferably residential, gathering of some size at which major issues could be presented and discussed. Something happens to people when they have a chance of meeting in a large company and finding that others share their interests in a wider view of the Church. We need a public demonstration in Scotland of the ecumenical reality which in fact exists.'[10] This idea, has, in fact, been included in the new arrangements; the first such 'Christian Gathering' was held in 1992 at Bearsden and the second is planned for Edinburgh in 1995.

Asked, when he was 83, to speak on 'Pleasure in old age', Robert tells us:

I live alone but also in community. My garden was too big so I sold my orchard to a couple with two young children and they built a bungalow. I had to build a fence to mark the divide but I built a gate in it. We come and go freely. There have been a dozen children living around me. I made it clear that I thought a fairly large garden was wasted if there were no children playing. So it has become a place they can enter when they want a change of scene. Unfortunately my two relaxations of

*hill-walking and gardening are no longer possible ... [but] how near
I still am to the countryside with its changing beauty. Without leaving
my room I can see the geese flying overhead into the hills. On four
side roads leading out of Biggar there are seats in the hedge at a mile
distance from the town .... I am all for sitting and walking on the
hills.*

*Television is a marvellous way of acquiring new knowledge with-
out the embarrassment of displaying ignorance! The continuity of faith
and fresh discoveries of faith provide a basis for the deepest pleasure. I
don't read much theology, but give me a provocative book every time –
one that jerks me out of my pious inattention! And old people still
have much to learn. I used to think that one day I should perhaps
arrive on a plateau of certainty, modified virtue and peace! All passion
spent .... As I realise my increasing dependence on human assistance
I come also to realise that God is the great enabler. My favourite doctrine
is Grace. Every day I use a modest phrase of Thomas á Kempis, 'O
merciful Jesus, give me your grace that it may be with me, that it may
labour with me, that it may persevere with me to the end'.*[11]

'It is not easy to avoid feeling that 84 years are enough, and yet
I have so many friends – old and new – that life seems full.' So
wrote Robert in 1983; and to another: 'When you hear I've died,
shout "Halleluja!"' Always prepared to accept the necessity for
change, however, he was called upon to make one last adjustment
when he sold his beloved Croftlands and moved to a small
modern bungalow across the lane. He bore the considerable
upheaval with his usual good grace.

In October he had an apparently successful operation for a
replacement hip joint but after only a few weeks in his new
home it was dislocated and he returned to hospital. 'It is good
news for the other patients,' a friend said. 'They will have a
really happy Christmas.' Early in the New Year of 1984, however, the kidney condition from which he suffered deteriorated
and he died on Friday the 13th of January in Edinburgh Royal
Infirmary.

The funeral on 17th January took place in one of Edinburgh's
rare periods of blizzard and blocked roads, but many struggled to
attend. Hans-Ruedi Weber flew from the WCC at Geneva to

bring their tribute to Robert as he passed, in Philip Potter's words, 'from life to life'. He reported that when he had rung the ailing Visser 't Hooft with the news of Robert's death, Wim had spoken only two sentences: 'Robert was a great centre of silence in the world. I cannot imagine the world without Robert.' Then he laid down the phone.[12]

In March two services of thanksgiving were held in Edinburgh and in London in order to accommodate the range of those who wished both to mourn and to celebrate. Once more the letters arrived – but this time to Steven. For the Edinburgh service Archie Craig wrote strong words, rather dauntingly phrased as instructions to a biographer!

The mature Robert was a world figure exerting a width and weight and quality of Christian influence unwielded by any other Scottish minister of religion for decades past.

Archie claimed that he found

... incarnated in Robert, a model of creative 20th century church-manship .... It might be called a three-tense churchmanship: it was rooted in an intimate and widely based knowledge of the Church's history, its development within, and its contribution to, the life of the world; it was closely engaged in the Church's current problems and tasks and, if necessary, controversies; above all, it was continually illuminated and searched and empowered by an unsparing and inspiring vision of the not-yet Church, of the Church-of-Christ-to-be, the Church which shall have entered upon the combined heritages of the denominations .... I never came away from any conversation with Robert without somehow feeling that the New Testament Gospel – in its warmth, its stringency, its momentum, its unlimited promise – had become more credible than ever through that contact.[13]

A year before his death, as part of the preparations for the WCC Assembly at Vancouver, Robert had been asked to write the text of the Scottish Council of Churches' 1983 meditation, 'Easter is Gospel'. It appeared anonymously, but is peculiarly appropriate as his last printed message.

The over-arching theme was 'Choose Life'. From the Palm Sunday reflections comes:

It was a mixed crowd with mixed motives, such as we often see on the television screen. But Jesus was at home among ordinary people. He belongs to the whole world .... He did not seek to make a display. He came on a borrowed donkey and slipped away later from the crowd .... For us to understand him we have to discard some of our conventional pictures and see him as the one who humbled himself for others.

From Good Friday:

On the Cross he broke the power of evil and opened the way to life for all .... Today we are coming to see the crucified Jesus in the sick and injured, in the deprived and powerless, in prisoners and exiles, in the handicapped and jobless, and in all those 'acquainted with grief'. In that setting Jesus reveals his humility and his compassion.

From East Sunday:

Jesus' publicly known friends had forsaken him. Two secret disciples plucked up courage to perform the last rites. It reminds us that Jesus is not the private possession of professing Christians. There are no limits to the range of his love, nor any human reckoning of the lives that love has touched.

And, in full, from Easter Day:

John 20:1-18, 30-31: 'I have seen the Lord.'

A loving woman's words galvanised the disciples. Her report led to the great cry of the Church: 'Christ is risen; he is risen indeed'. Jesus is available, far more available, forever available to all humanity. The drift of mankind towards its own destruction, and the destruction of its environment, is not the last word of history. Easter denies that. Indeed the assurance of a risen Lord provides the basis for positive striving towards justice and peace. In his name, like the early church, we go forward.

These are written that you may believe that Jesus is the Christ, the Son of God, and that believing you may have life in his name.

We often believe in such a half-hearted way that we do not receive the promised life. Perhaps we think that eternal life belongs to the future. So it does, but the good news is that life of the same texture begins now. It is new every Easter, new every morning. We do not have to deserve it, simply to choose it.[14]

Notes to Chapter 12

1   Mackie Papers, Edinburgh.
2   Ibid.
3   Reported by Eleanor Jackson who wrote a large part of her biography of William Paton, *Red Tape and the Gospel*, whilst staying at Croftlands.
4   WCC Archives, Ecumenical Centre Library, Geneva.
5   Notes on a Journey to Wick. September 1976: Mackie Papers.
6   Eightieth Birthday Tributes: ibid.
7   Letter from Robert to Visser 't Hooft, 24.5.1979: WCC Archives.
8   Letter from Robert to Visser 't Hooft, 8.11.1979: ibid.
9   WCC Archives.
10 Dunblane Archives.
11 'Pleasure in Old Age': Mackie Papers.
12 Mackie Papers.
13 Ibid.
14 Dunblane Archives.

List of Abbreviations

ACTS	*Action of Churches Together in Scotland*
BB	*Boys' Brigade*
BCC	*British Council of Churches*
CIMADE	*French Agency working in France on behalf of the ICA Department Comité Intermouventaire par l'Aide aux Evacuées*
HLI	*Highland Light Infantry*
ICA	*Inter-Church Aid*
IMC	*International Missionary Council*
ISS	*International Student Service*
IVF	*Inter-Varsity Fellowship*
PLO	*Palestine Liberation Organisation*
SCEA	*Scottish Churches' Ecumenical Association*
SCM	*Student Christian Movement*
USCC	*United Student Christian Council*
WCC	*World Council of Churches*
WSCF	*World's Christian Student Federation*
YMCA	*Young Men's Christian Association*
YWCA	*Young Women's Christian Association*

Index of Names